THE SPLENDOR OF **SEEING**
AND THE **MAGIC** OF **TOUCH**

THE SPLENDOR OF SEEING AND THE MAGIC OF TOUCH

On Sensuality-Sexuality in Loving Relationships

RICHARD J. ALAPACK

iUniverse, Inc.
Bloomington

THE SPLENDOR OF SEEING AND THE MAGIC OF TOUCH
On Sensuality-Sexuality in Loving Relationships

iUniverse books may be ordered through booksellers or by contacting:

iUniverse
1663 Liberty Drive
Bloomington, IN 47403
www.iuniverse.com
1-800-Authors (1-800-288-4677)

ISBN: 978-1-4697-0937-6 (sc)
ISBN: 978-1-4697-0938-3 (ebk)

Printed in the United States of America

iUniverse rev. date: 01/05/2012

CONTENTS

ABOUT THE AUTHOR

Richard J. Alapack, Ph. D. holds as mattering most the love bonds with his family and the relationships with true blue friends. Chili, his beloved wife, comes first and foremost. Then, he has four splendidly talented children: two lovely women, his daughter, Nicole and step-daughter, Minh Trang—nicknamed Tara—and two handsome sons, Richard and Orion. Furthermore, he is blessed with the Light, Life, and Love of three granddaughters: Nicole's three bright and beautiful daughters, Sophie, Olivia, and Natalie Grace.

Richard works as an Associate Professor of Psychology at the Norwegian University of Science and Technology. His recent books are *White Hot-True Blue* (2010), *Christopher and the balance beam* (2011) written with Olivia P. Stasio and Sophie E. Stasio, *Sorrow's Profiles: Death, Grief and Crisis in the Family* (2010) and *Love's Pivotal Relationships: The Chum, First Love, Outlaw and the Intimate Partner* (2007). With this current publication, *The Splendor of Seeing and the Magic of Touch*, these volumes cover the spectrum of life and death, love and sorrow, sensuality-sexuality, and the life spiral from infancy to old age. In a nutshell, Richard wants to showcase a human psychology fit for this age of "Occupy Wall Street" and the "Arab Spring." Revolutionary protestors that want to give back to the people are poised to replace the "breathtakingly greedy" business-industrial-military-governmental complex that has co-created a world divided into 1% that are stuffed and the far-too-many that are starving. A piece of qualitative algebra expresses Richard's standpoint: Power fades, money vanishes, fame is fickle, and ambition is foolish; only love lasts.

ACKNOWLEDGEMENTS

Gratefully, I acknowledge the following publishers for granting me permission to use in a modified version articles that I have previously published and have re-framed, added to and deleted from in this manuscript.

I credit Taylor and Francis for the following two publications:

Alapack, R. J. 2011. Under siege: A woman's beauty and health. *The Humanistic Psychologist*, **39**(04), 366-374.

Alapack, R.J. 1991. Adolescent first kiss. *The Humanistic Psychologist*. 19(1), 48-67.

I credit Mary Ann Liebert, Inc., Publishers for:

Alapack, R.J. M. Flydal Blichfeldt, and Å. Elden. 2005. Flirting on the Internet and the hickey: A hermeneutic. *CyberPsychology & Behavior* 8(1), 52-61

And I credit Wiley-Blackwell for:

Alapack, R. J. 2009. The epiphany of female flesh: A phenomenological hermeneutic of popular fashion. *Journal of Popular Culture*, 42 (6). 977-1003.

ORIENTING COMMENTS

Warm and commonplace sensual-sexual phenomena comprise the core of this book. Specifically, the assortment of topics includes peekaboo, a game played by an infant and her 'mothering one', the children's games of hide and seek and tag, the adolescent and adult experiences of the blush, kissing, the hickey, and the caress, flirting on the Internet, and encounters with fashion and beauty. These phenomena showcase the powerful place that the primary senses of vision and touch occupy within our loving relationships. Who of us have not played these delightful children's games? Who has not had unforgettable "moments" of kissing and caressing? Who has not been awed by fashion and dazzled by beauty? The content of this book concern us all.

The splendor of seeing and the magic of touch are basic experiences, part and parcel of everyday life. Touch touches everything. Nevertheless, the publishing industry takes them for granted. Social scientific researchers, enamored with theory, models, and methods, overlook them. Trade books, even though they aim at lively engagement and emotional appeal, nevertheless rarely make them theme. This book brings these simple, seemingly trite and trivial phenomena to center stage. It offers descriptions and reflections that showcase their relevance to us all. It suits to give a preview of coming attractions.

Play

We humans play. Spontaneous, free play is as natural as the sun coming up. We play for play's sake. Not surprisingly, *homo ludens* has been put forth as the essential definition of our humanness: man, the player.

Games

A child's game is a game in its own right. Infants, children, youth, and grownups participate in games for the sheer fun of playing. Play requires no ulterior motive and typically has none. Play is first and foremost enjoyment. But a game is never just a game. Beyond mere bodily pleasure and interpersonal enjoyment, games generate other spin-offs. We humans concoct games consciously for social purposes and less than consciously to serve our psychological economy. Just like all specifically human activities such as work, sexuality, prayer, and so forth, many layers of meaning permeate play.

Peekaboo

Arguably, peekaboo is the most basic or original game. Peekaboo concerns the disappearance and reappearance of "Mother." In the game, baby and mother giggle about her vanishing and re-emergence. Its dynamic structure guarantees that she will re-appear again each and every time that she disappears from sight. The game is foolproof. Mother always comes back. Participating in this vivid drama helps the wee one to manage the childhood anxiety about separation and abandonment.

Natural Scientific Psychology: Research with Peekaboo

Mainstream psychological research on peekaboo does not study it as a phenomenon in its own right. The experimental approach uses it to test a legion of other developmental variables. But researchers ignore the meaning of the game to the infant, to the mother, and to their richly complex and precious bond. A peek at how the ruling paradigm addresses peekaboo exposes the essential picture of the mainstream approach to all psychological phenomena.

Hide and Seek

All over the globe, preadolescents play hide and seek. It is a prime choice of kids between the ages of five and twelve. A specifically anxious predicament of this age is lost-and-found. Hide and seek is a particularly brilliant game because it cannot fail. It always dissipates the anxiety about being lost, guarantees the security of belonging and safety. If a lad or lassie should become lost, or foolishly tries to hide away, someone will always find him or her.

Playing Tag: First Erotic Touch

At puberty the fledgling adolescent begins to look at the other with different eyes. The new gaze seizes upon the explicitly sexual aspects of the surroundings and also spies life's mysterious differences. The urge to touch and be touched by the other becomes strong. Playing 'tag', as simple yet as profoundly metaphorical a game as imaginable, involves the first erotic touch. It copes splendidly with nascent anxieties associated with sensual-sexual touch. The gender differences in sharing the first touch are striking. My narrative illustrates them.

The Blush

Mark Twain pens a pithy but truthful line: "Man is the only animal that blushes, or who needs to." **Blushing is a concrete symbol of the early adolescent predicament.** A young boy and young girl growing into sexual manhood and womanhood, lock eyes. Their shared stare communicates the message; I-know-that-you-know-that-I know. In awkwardness, they blush. The blush is an evanescent beam of nascent sensuality.

Adolescent First Kiss

Who cannot remember the time when whether to give or receive our first real kiss was a living question? Many of us waited with longing that first touch of another's lips. Others dreaded it with an all-consuming irrational fear. Still others found ourselves precipitously plunged into the heretofore strange situation. Some of us do not remember it at all. Each initiation into kissing is a story in itself. How did we negotiate that unprecedented "moment" wherever it happened, or whatever our age, or whether we were eager, overwhelmed, agonized, graced, or stunned? Our adolescent first kiss is the gateway to romance.

The Meaning of Kissing in General

The kiss conveys quintessential intimacy. The kiss is touch. It is often sexual, but not always. No sexual act is more intimate than kissing. The kiss is more personally expressive than intercourse. It can mean more than a climax. Because why? A kiss must be reciprocated, must be returned. A kiss that is not bi-lateral is a failure, an aborted attempt. The kiss cannot be faked. Either we are 'in' it or it is empty and cold. There is no place to hide while kissing and no way to camouflage heartfelt emotions. A kiss is truth-telling. It starts and ends our most significant relationships.

The Hickey

A hickey is a blatant mark on some part of the human body made by one person putting her or his mouth on another person's skin, biting or sucking for a protracted period of time. It is hard to pinpoint a phenomenon better suited than the hickey to express the adolescent's ambiguous predicament of being troubled by lust. Its indecisive and equivocal carnality perturbs an awkward youth. A painful whirlpool or a situational vortex easily draws in a young man or woman suddenly and surprisingly bedecked with hickeys. The hickey is an embarrassing badge of burgeoning sexuality.

Although seemingly trite and trivial, the meaning of a hickey is much broader that the mere trading of the "bite." The phenomenon belongs to the larger groupings of: 1) other bodily marks and stains; 2) social-cultural rituals, rites, traditions, and folklore; 3) and various historical practices of flesh-branding during spectacles of public punishment.

The Caress

The difference between being "caressed" and being "pawed" reveals much about the many different possible types of sexual encounters and about the ambiguous relationship between lust and love. The caress is the miraculous movement of tenderness. The sensible flesh communes intimately with sensible flesh. Pawing, on the other hand, is a 'hit-and-run' touch, the movement either of lust, need, selfish pleasure, or thrill-seeking.

Flirting Online

Nowadays, erotic behavior in cyberspace is customary. Online dating is a multi-million dollar industry. What is its appeal? What sustains it? This chapter presents a picture of romantic-erotic action in cyberspace and addresses the essential difference between flirting by text with flirting face-to-face in the flesh

Fashion

Is not fashion an ever-present pivot? Around it swings the door between sensual-sexual lure and popular culture, Fashion reveals the social climate, the contemporary political climate, and the historical "moment." The weave of wardrobe and skin, makeup and hairstyles, perfume, jewelry, and accessories holds a powerful sway particularly over our youth. I do an expose of the "bare belly button" look as a lead into the history of woman's fashion throughout modernity.

Beauty

A woman's beauty and her health are under siege in our postmodern world. A warped pursuit of it as commodity also endangers her physical-psycho-spiritual health. The marriage between Late Capitalism and the Patriarchy menaces women in the concrete shape of various industries: cosmetic, fashion, aesthetic medicine, pharmaceutical, marketing, the media, bodily modification, diet. They fabricate a counterfeit image of beauty, indoctrinate that nobody is beautiful enough, and tender expensive treatment to enhance appearance. Mainstream scholars and professionals, sadly, shelter the siege.

Final Punctuation: Psyche-in-flesh

This chapter distinguishes in detail the objective, anatomical-physiological body that natural science studies exclusively as the body, and the lived, subjective, experienced body that co-creates our sensual-sexual "moments."

Basic Presupposition

All we have in life are "moments." Most are one-in-a-row and once only. We experience the "moment" and either it dies on the vine or develops into an encounter, a meeting, an episode, or eventually builds into a relationship that might last a lifetime. This book starts with the precious instants. I do not cater to the rational bias of western thought that the idea or concept is most 'real'. In this book, I privilege the "moment" as the basic building block of knowledge. I italicize it throughout.

To Whom Do I Pitch The Book?

I have written this book for the salt-of-the-earth people. The ordinary reader is literate and educated, but not especially enamored with the arcane erudite vocabulary of so-called specialists and experts. Hence, I do not write for the disciplinary academics and professionals that are mostly obsessed with method and addicted to theories and their pet models. Kierkegaard calls them "bag peerers" Nietzsche names them "scholarly oxen." Nowadays, they belong to "clubs" with their own rules and a peculiar language with which they write 'love-letters' to one another and call it 'scholarship'. In unfolding the phenomena of this book, deliberately I eschew abstract language tied to conceptual ideology. Equally, I avoid the vocabulary of introductory to psychology books that basically aim to socialize the reader to the cognitive-behavioral discipline now in vogue. In my descriptive narratives about everyday life experiences, the human and personally idiosyncratic meanings of commonplace phenomena concern me. I privilege the language of daily life. That does not mean, however, that my vocabulary is simplistic. The last thing I want to do is to condescend to you. In my judgment, the academic journal caters arrogantly only to the initiated, and both the textbook and the trade book industries so write down that they spoon-feed the reader. In tune with an educational system severely accused of "dumming down" America, neither the textbook nor a typical trade book challenges our command of language. My granddaughters who have coauthored a book with me, twelve year old, Sophie and ten year old, Olivia show me levels of understanding of words that put much of published writing to shame. So I pull no punches in using whatever word best describes the 'moment' and to communicate its sense. I would rather that you complain of having to consult a dictionary too many times while reading me than to hear you moan, "This book is too superficial."

Definite philosophical and psychological viewpoints underpin this book. And an array of qualitative methods leads to my word-portraits and generate my knowledge-claims. I honor the contribution to my work of Professor Amedeo Giorgi whose seminal and decisive thinking has given me access to the rich treasures of existentialism, phenomenology and hermeneutics. In *The splendor of seeing and the magic of touch* I bracket the fullness of their concepts in order to let shine the phenomena of the book. I cannot avoid certain technical terms, but I keep them to a minimum. I hope I have not compromised the common touch. Throughout the book, I reference other writers to give due credit to authors and to prick the interest of the reader to check them out. Whenever I use a fifty cent word, I immediately give the nickel alternative.

With my mind warmed by my heart I write the narratives, portraits, and parables. I weave them with heartlines seeped in passion and tenderness and stained by tears of joy and sorrow. The knowledge-claims I share are objective precisely because I do not bypass but go through my subjectivity. The knowledge is pre-eminently personal, engaged, concerned, and earnest. My writing fails miserably if my heartlines do not trigger thoughts about your own experiences and meanings, and provoke dwelling upon your feelings and memories,

CHAPTER ONE

The Body at Play: Peekaboo

First and foremost, our body moves. Before it behaves, our body stirs and freely meanders about. It plays. The human organism, in addition to being an anatomical-physiological object, is a living body, a dynamically unified and meaning-creating subject.

One does not have to ascribe to the notion that man is "the player," *homo lumens*, to affirm the primacy of free play (Huizinga, 1944/1955). Behavior, which mainstream psychology throughout modernity until today makes the privileged term to characterize humanness, is only one way among many that depicts activity. This book unfolds from the perspective of holism. It eschews the reduction of the totality of human comportment to behavior, a mere sliver of the whole human person.

Games

A child's game is a game in its own right. Infants, children, youth, and grownups participate in games for the sheer fun of playing. Play for play's sake is indeed the basic purpose of the involvement. Play requires no ulterior motive and typically has none. Scholars and researchers should never reduce play to anything less than itself. The history of play in the western world, however, reveals that doers and thinkers have not only reduced it but presented it negatively as an activity that requires justification (Alapack, 1972). The classic legitimization argues that play is the child's form of work. My presupposition is clear and forceful: play is first and foremost enjoyment.

1

But a game is never just a game. Beyond mere bodily pleasure and interpersonal enjoyment games generate other spin-offs. We humans concoct games consciously for social purposes and less than consciously to serve our psychological economy. Just like all specifically human activities, work, sexuality, prayer, and so forth, many layers of meaning permeate play.

Ordinary commonplace games allow youngsters to work off worries or anxieties and to handle certain developmental milestones. That is why different games interest different chronological age groups. For the same reason, a given game waxes within a group's repertoire and then wanes as the children crossover into another developmental era.

Playing Peekaboo

Lickety-split, here comes an example. Peekaboo is an amazingly simple and ingeniously profound game. Bruner and Sherwood (1976, 277-78) write that it ranks as one of the most universal forms of play between adults and infants. Why universal and so enduring? Whence the game's power?

Peekaboo is a rock bottom "rudimentary" game (Phillips, 1967, 66). It depicts the heart and soul of the interaction of the primary I-Thou bond (Buber, 1958). The infant and her mother or a significant 'mothering one' play it. From the infant's side, the phenomenon indexes the deepest psychological issue in relation to her most important caretakers. For the mother playing the game is a fundamental way to engage and to enjoy her dependent wee one.

Existential Method: A Father-Grandfather Gives Eye-Witness Living Proof

I offer a first person singular account of peekaboo seeped in passion and tenderness and rooted in my fragile experience and flawed expertise. I give prima facie evidence from the standpoint of an eyewitness, an implicated insider. I give testimony of the heart joined with the head.

Starting nearly forty years ago, I have played peekaboo with my daughter, Nicole, and with my sons, Rich and Orion. I also watched them play with their mothers. More recently, I played peekaboo with two of my three granddaughters, Sophie (age 12 years, 4 months) and Olivia (10 years, 5 months old) as I write this (December 13, 2011). I was working in Norway during the time-frame that the family played the game with Natalie Grace (two years, ten months old). But Nicole and her sisters told me stories of their enjoyment.

As both a participant and an eye-witness, I have been blessed over the decades to enjoy, savor, and mull over my oft-repeated experiences and observations. Originally, I jotted down notes on the dynamics of the "gut play" that I lived through. Today, I tap into the interactions of the mother-infant dyad that I witnessed. Those 'moments', reflected until ripe, constitute the raw data of my knowledge-claims.

Aristotle writes that it is a mark of ignorance of a seeker after truth and wisdom to try to prove what is self-evident and needs no proof (Heidegger, 1969/1993, 449). A Turkish Proverb says, "The heart's testimony is better than a thousand witnesses." My approach to peekaboo is interested, concerned, earnest, and in depth. The passionately tender picture I offer of it emerges out of my self-reflective search.

A Psychological Portrait of Peekaboo

What is the basic psychological . . . psychological value of peekaboo in the life of the infant? By seemingly stuttering above on the 'p' word, I purposefully want to accent that I seek an in-depth and soulful meaning of the game, i.e., its personal, idiosyncratic, subjective significance. The following portrait addresses the depth-life question: what place does playing the game with "mother" serve within the psychological economy of the infant's life?

Essential Picture of Peekaboo

In a nutshell, peekaboo concerns the disappearance and reappearance of "Mother." It is a game of giggling about her vanishing and re-emergence. Its dynamic structure guarantees that she will re-appear again whenever she disappears from sight. Mother, who has gone away, always comes back. Participating in this vivid drama helps the wee one to manage childhood anxieties. How so?

The plot of the play is mum's thinly veiled disappearance. "There are . . . no stated rules for the game. There are however, some definite "requirements" (Phillips, 1967, 66). These requirements are elegantly simple and chock full of significance. Momma either covers herself, or covers baby's face, or hides from baby's view, under a blanket—often the baby's own favorite one, "Blankie", what D.W. Winnicott (1953) names her "transitional object," one that stands in for the "mother." During the brief time of hiding—just a few scant seconds—mom sustains contact by makings sounds or saying something to heighten the excitement of anticipation (Bruner & Sherwood, 1976). "Where is Sophie?" "I can't see you, Olivia!" "Is Richie hiding on mommy?" "Where, oh where can Orion be?" "Nicole, where are you? I've looked *everywhere* for you!"

Mother's absent-presence both prolongs and sustains the infant's suspense. Spontaneously and intuitively, mother manages the episode. She 'knows' her infant. So she knows how to draw the fine line between "make believe" and "real" events. In lived time, not measured duration, she knows how long her precious baby can comfortably 'tolerate' the interval of anticipation. At the right "moment," she pops out from her hiding place. "I see you," she crows softly but with enthusiasm. And she lays her eyes on her precious baby, wearing a large smile. As she laughs, her ample presence fills the empty hole that temporarily had punctuated baby's life space. To add to the richness of the "moment," she tickles baby, too, in her little ribs or under her chin at the sensitive spot on her neck. Even before being tickled, with eyes wide open and expectant, baby giggles in anticipation of being touched.

Since it is cardinal to the significance of this game without rules, it bears repeating that mothers are incredibly adept at budgeting time. They cradle anticipation, use it to build a bridge over the 'moment' of disappearance, and with equal savvy re-cross that bridge at the 'right time' to forestall fidgeting, fretting, or tears.

For example, if mother holds a cover over her face, out of the corner of her eye she peeks at her little girl, creating a scaffold to hold her in the ambiguous few eye-blinks of the event. Or perhaps she lets part of herself show. Maybe she whispers audibly, or squeals, or giggles. The infant giggles in response. The tension surrounding the disappearance dissipates the instant mom re-appears. Pleasure and gratification replace it. Once mother does magic with her fingers, the infant will giggle even more joyously. Then they giggle together.

There are lots of ways to play the game. While "drying the child's hair after a bath," mother turns the episode into a game of peekaboo (Bruner & Sherwood, 1976, 278-279). Or mommy ducks below the level of the child's highchair, or slips out of sight when the child is lying in her crib. Within the flexible structure of the game, that allows for a plethora of variations, mom and baby might take turns at initiating action. My daughter, Nicole, told me that Natalie, her daughter, at the age of ten months took an agent's stance concerning the game. In a spontaneous 'moment', she covers herself with a blanket and then pulls it off, saying with a 'pleased-as-punch' smile, "Peek." Then she hands the blanket to her mother.

Whatever the variation, at the 'right' time mother says "Boo," calls the infant's name, or in some way brings the episode to a close. Especially when the child is a bit older, mom might scoot out of the nursery. "Peek-a-boo," she will holler at a distance and then burst back into the room singing as she runs, "I see you!" And again her eyes will caress the baby who waits with bated breath to see her. This time mother will scoop the baby out of her crib and carry her downstairs saying, "Lunch time. Peanut butter and jam! Yum-yum! Yoghurt too! Bananas and lots of fruit! Oh, let's see what kind of fruit we have in the 'frig. Lucky baby! Raspberries, your favorite! Mommy just loves you so much. Mommy is going to eat you up!"

Then she does gobble up her precious little one, covering her with kisses while plopping her into her highchair and strapping her safely in. Time to eat now; the game ends, naturally . . . until the next time.

Mommy will say "I love you" over and over again. She will never tire. She will kiss baby, kiss, kiss, and kiss. Kisses and touches are infinite. We never fall short of them; we can never give them all away. Touch touches everything. These two are a nursing couple; they are symbiotic partners. Mother never runs out of kisses, snuggles, or hugs. Baby's cheeks will never wear out.

When the child is approximately two years old, the age limit at which playing the game stops making phenomenological sense, a sophisticated variation of words suits: "I'm hiding / I'm hiding away from you / don't look for me / don't find me / you'll be sorry if your do . . . Boo!" To play peekaboo, however, only one basic act is necessary. All mother needs to do is cover her eyes and remain quiet; just pretend to be hiding; pretend to be gone. Because why?

For a little child Mother's closed or absent eyes and silence are significant disappearances. Ultimately, the act of creating the absence of the eyes and feigning stone cold silence assumes the pose of Death. Peekaboo, therefore, re-enacts the drama of separation and death. Is there a more vivid description of what it means to be dead than to say that the tongue no longer speaks and that the eyes are missing because the light in them has gone out? (Alapack, 2010, 99).

Smiling and laughing are crucial to mother-infant play even from a purely experimental standpoint (Fogel, Dickson, Hus, Messinger, Melson-Goens & Nwokah. 1997). The voice and face are specifically pivotal to playing peekaboo (Fernald & O' Neill, 1993), but superficial experimental findings cannot pinpoint the reason. Sensitivity to the existential predicament of the infant is necessary to understand what's at stake. And that predicament is necessary for understanding all facets of human development.

Reflections: Premature Human Birth

The predicament roots in the fundamental anthropological fact that *the human infant is born prematurely*. Thus, the infant is absolutely dependent upon a human bond. After birth, our animal brothers and sisters can survive relatively quickly on their own. Instincts 'kick in'. The animal can fend for self. Human life, however, is based upon consciousness not instincts. The infant requires momma's soothing, caressing, resonant voice and radiant eyes. She desperately needs momma's commanding words and her sharp sight. The little one must be "held and handled" by the competent hands and the insightful, empathic, and intuitive vision of maternal wisdom. The baby integrates and personifies because "mother" loves her (Winnicott, 1965). Absolutely hopelessly and helplessly dependent, the child needs to see mother, at least intermittently, and needs to know that mother sees her. "The eyes do not shine, they speak (Levinas, 1961/1969). "Peek-a-boo, I see you."

Fittingly, we humans have created a game so that the infant can practice overcoming separation anxiety about losing her primary caregiver, Jean Piaget, (1936/1992) demonstrates that the emergence of "object constancy," the awareness that an object removed from sight still exists, starts between ages six to eight months. Object constancy is indispensable to the infant's mastery of separation anxiety. It is a vital achievement for the growing child finally to take for granted that Mother is present-in-her-absence. It is a sign of a healthy, relaxed, and secure child that she can tolerate mommy being temporary gone. Winnicott (1965) says that the child, by intermittingly "checking back" to assure mother's presence, develops sophisticated aloneness. Jean-Paul Sartre (1943/1966) informs us that absence is a not just a lack, a nothingness, but a mode of being present.

Mother is not omnipresent or omniscient. It is fundamental to the authentic sense of freedom that the child realizes that mamma cannot read her mind. There is a secret part of me that mamma never sees (Elkin, 1972). I don't have to see her all the time either. Genuine freedom in life demands that mother does not have eyes in the back of her head. Even though mother cannot always see me—and never sees me perfectly—nevertheless she does see me well enough concerning what matters most: consistent, reliable care. Peekaboo is the game that repeats that message over and over again. "I. See. You . . . And I love you!"

The Importance of Touch

Within the game, the touch of the eyes and hands are intimate. It is also sensual. It is sexual, too. Sigmund Freud (1905) clarified the connection between seeing and sexual arousal by using the phrase lust-in-looking—*schaulust* in his homey German language. In peekaboo, sexuality is only minimally present—in approximately the sense that breast feeding is sexual. That is, sexuality is only at the margin and very far removed from the thematic act of playing the game.

The game itself moves on a pivot of sensual-sexual-spiritual desire. Søren Kierkegaard (1884/1980) says desire is present from the start of life, within the age of "innocence." Within his anthropological framework, desire must be present between the infant-mother, the symbiotic partners or "nursing couple", because the human destiny is to become spirit. "In the state of innocence, man is not merely an animal, for then, if for even a single moment in his life he were merely an animal, he would never become a man" (1844/1980, 39).

Desire at this stage is undifferentiated, indefinite, and present only in premonition of itself. The infant lives immediately at-one with the mother and has not yet separated from her surroundings. She has not yet come to self-consciousness. So desire and the desired are united. It's a magical world, a uni-verse, a turning towards one. In peekaboo, we witness desire awakened, charmed, and captivated by what it desires. The game adumbrates sensual and spiritual desire to come in the future.

In hide and seek, the next game I investigate, the dynamics of touch differ. Touch is not as plentiful or nearly as intimate as the mother-child love-play during peek-a-boo. In hide and seek, sensual-sexual touch is part of the field that surrounds the theme. Finally, in tag, the third game I consider, erotic touch is precisely the theme.

The Primacy of the Bond

The game of peekaboo is fundamentally and radically interpersonal or relational. The bond between the mother and infant sponsors the game's value and significance. It manifests the incredibly natural emotional exchange between the infant and mother. All emotions that emerge during the play veer toward the bond and turn to what is happening between both partners. The infant is immediately at-one with her mother. The emotions at stake for the infant are anxiety in the face of mother's disappearance, the gleeful excitement of anticipation while awaiting her re-appearance, and the delight in the 'moment' she returns a-crowing, "Peek-a-boo, I see you." Without the vital bond between the two participants, it is absurdly abstract to talk about a game of peekaboo

The psychological portrait presented above does not juggle stock phrases or clichés such as "Out-of-sight, out-of-mind," "Absence makes the heart grow fonder." After the healthy, growing, and thriving child discovers object-constancy, things continue to exist even when they are outside her field of vision. The child learns that she is not the center of the universe. The existence of something does not depend upon my perceiving it. People are not swallowed up or siphoned off the face of the earth. Ma loves me, but she has a life separate from me, too. Ties of affection do not dissolve in the face of physical absence. Love and care are not totally contingent upon the 'here-ness' of space and the 'now-ness' of time. Momma's love remains as solid as the rock of Gibraltar even if it is drenched in fog or draped by darkness. Care endures, even when the love-object is gone from sight. The game gives the core assurance, "I am well loved! I play under a rainbow." Mother lets it shine like a beacon of light: "Peek-a-boo!" I . . . see . . . you. I . . . love . . . you. I'm coming home soon. I am coming back to you. Trust me. Trust our love-bond. The chord that joins us together stretches far and wide, without snapping . . . even if I am an ocean away!"

Even death won't part us.

CHAPTER TWO

Natural Science Psychology
Looks at Peekaboo

Actually, it looks with skewed vision. This chapter differs 180 degrees from all the rest of the book. You can easily ignore it and go on to the next chapter describing hide and seek. Mainstream psychological researchers show scant interest in the game of peekaboo qua game. Laboratory researchers experiment with peekaboo, but they do not study it. They use it to test a legion of other developmental psychological variables. In the process, they ignore the meaning of the game to the infant, to the mother, and to their richly complex and precious bond.

The purpose of chapter is to lay bare this important research 'choice' that loses the essential meanings of the game. Mainstream researchers follow the "received" tradition of "known standards," falling under the sway of the natural scientific paradigm. Therefore, they remain beholden to its privileged quantitative methods, modes, and procedures, and to its forms and formats for making knowledge-claims.

It is not my intention in this chapter to catalogue or summarize the reported findings in the literature. I merely bring to view the essential picture of the standardized way that the ruling paradigm addresses peekaboo and all Lifeworld phenomena. I make this critical expose once in this chapter rather than repeating the same critique in subsequent chapters.

This chapter gives you a perfect contrast between two views of the science of psychology. It pits my picture of peekaboo, drawn with earthy heartlines and written with the ordinary educated reader in mind, against a neutral, objective, abstract description crafted in arid prose and written in disciplinary jargon and terminology to please colleagues and appease Gatekeepers.

Mainstream scientists, intellectuals, academics, and professionals quibble, quarrel, and disagree about precision of conceptualization and the particulars of execution. But they share agreement that the natural scientific program is the proper way to practice science. The entire rational community considers it the standard for judging knowledge-claims. Gatekeepers within various system-sanctioned sub-systems reject as non-scientific any research that disregards accepted processes and procedures, forms and formats. Those who wield power and hold the purse strings decide the recognition, acceptance, and dissemination of scientific knowledge. Power dictates knowledge (Foucault, 1975/1979).

Integrity demands that I confront the mainstream approach. I criticize it for overlooking concrete, raw experience, personal meaning, and precious individuality. I chastise the dominant paradigm for icing out whatever remains outside its purview. It would be reverse myopia and hypocrisy to ignore the ruling approach. But I hereby make no noble gesture. I hope to garner your appreciation of my alternative standpoint by juxtaposing my picture of peekaboo and one that merely uses it to serve theoretical issues. By not just parroting the literature but criticizing it severely, perhaps I'll convince one of you that power and money artificially prop up psychology's ruling paradigm. Natural science psychology dupes our culture in the same manner that Han Christian Andersen's classic tale reveals. The Dane puts into the mouth of an innocent boy the illuminating cry: The Emperor is wearing no clothing.

Mainstream Experimental Studies of Peekaboo

Specifically, what is the style of the mainstream research on peekaboo? They use the game as an "example" either to explain a legion of cognitive, emotional, or behavioral variables pertinent to their theoretical models or "to predict certain behaviors"

(Ogino, Ooide, Watanabe, & Asada, 2007, 117). Developmental psychologists use the game to experiment with other infant behaviors or to "examine" the broad spectrum of "infant abilities" such as "communication" (Ogino, Ooide, Watanabe, & Asada, 2007, 116), or "the perception of emotion expressions" (Montague & Walker-Andrews.(2001, 826; 831), or "expectations in play" (Parrott & Gleitman, 1989, 291), or "the learning of rule structures" (Bruner and Sherwood (1976. 277-278). These studies generate neutral, detached, behavioral, and technical facts; they provide objective information that support or contest prevalent views and theoretical models of infant development. In the best sense, these findings incrementally advance the field. But they do not reveal the heartfelt picture of the game. They demonstrate that the most easily measured and quantified material is of least significance in human terms. The heart, psyche, and spirit go missing. Unaddressed also remains the basic psychological question that my portraits and heartlines respond to: *what place does playing the game with "mother" serve within the psychological economy of the infant's life?*

Age-related preoccupations

Age-grading is an obsession among developmental psychologists. Not surprisingly, age is a hotly debated topic in research on peekaboo. Concerning age-related variables, various theorists have noted important shifts during the second half of the first year of life. Piaget's object constancy is one. Another is Jacques Lacan's (1966/1977) "mirror stage," the "moment" when the infant and her caregiver play with gleeful satisfaction (*jouissance*) that she recognizes her self-image in the mirror. A chimpanzee, incredibly more sophisticated at the same age in terms of sensory-motor capabilities, lacks the capacity to share the mirror-"moment." The depressive position emerges at this time, too (Klein, 1975). An infant does not show signs of despondency as a result of a protracted separation from her primary caregiver until six to eight months (Spitz, 1965).

Not surprisingly, some research contradicts the exactness of this marker event. Montague and Walker-Andrews (2001, 837) "provide strong evidence that 4-month-old infants are differentially responsive to composite facial/vocal expressions of emotion in a familiar, naturalistic setting." Entering this debate does not concern us. I just cite these studies to show the flavor of the research and to exemplify its style. Theoretical debate takes center stage. The texture of the game is off-stage. It only shows to exemplify the point that the one debating wants to make. Within which time-frames does the infant "become sensitive to the regular behavior of their caregivers (Ogino, Ooide, Watanabe, & Asada, 2007, 116), or gain "the ability to discriminate expressions" (Montague, Walker-Andrews, (2001, 826), or is capable of reciprocal play, or is acoustically and/or facially sensitive to surprise and happy so part and parcel of peekaboo?

Is this age-grading genuinely useful? Data about dates help explain variables that intrigue researchers. But in a radical sense, getting to the heart of the matter of peekaboo, to the place it serves in an infant's psychological economy, does not hinge upon age. In life outside the laboratory, the mother and infants share "moments." 'Moments' are all we have in life; but shared "moments" build into episodes, encounters, and into deep and abiding relationships (Alapack, 2010, 11). The loving mother trades in those "moments" day by day, week by week, and year by year. It is the relationship between her and her infant that sheds light on what matters, not the ticks of the clock.

Deleting the human

Very disturbingly, I found research procedures which minimize or disregard the primary mother-infant bond. Some designs legitimize leaving out completely either party. 'They' substitute, for instance, a surrogate partner for mother or a robot for baby. An oft-copied experimental design justifies purposefully deceiving vulnerable infants. I will return to this matter below.

I first pose a basic question. Does it matter if an infant playing peekaboo plays with her own mother, with a "mothering one," or with a familiar, natural caregiver such as father, older sister, or grandparent? Will any woman-robot fit the bill? If you judge that any co-player is equivalent to the infant's mother or another normal, natural partner, then this book is not your cup of tea. In my portrait of peekaboo, no experimenter or paid graduate assistant can substitute for these natural partners, Take out the mother or the infant or both, and you are playing scientific game. You are not playing peekaboo.

Routinely, however, experimentalists find it convenient to bracket the living mother-infant couple. Montague and Walker-Andrews (2001, 829) initially observed mothers and babies playing peekaboo both in their own homes and in the laboratory. But their "new look" and "new methodology" replaced the natural mother in the experimental situation with a female "experimenter"-"investigator." During the trials, the biological mother sat behind the infant. Presumably, in the minds of the research team she just blended in with the woodwork. In that situation, however, she would not transmute unto neutral or inert dead wood. You don't believe, do you, that the infant just 'tuned out' her mother and acted like a perfectly trained, unbiased research "subject"? The presence of the 'real' mother, close enough to see, smell, or sense never transmutes into neutral background or dead wood.

Nevertheless, the researchers allege that their paradigm "capitalized on the *naturalistic*, familiar dyadic interactions in the infant's world . . . gaining information more refined and precise than what *"less naturalistic paradigms"* yield, ones that use "slides, photographs or videotapes" (Montague and Walker-Andrews, 2001, 836, my emphasis). Two paragraphs above in their text, however, these two scientists proudly disclaim using the natural mother-infant team and declare their design more effective because "It allowed greater control over the fidelity and accuracy of an expression than would a *purely naturalistic design*" (Montague and Walker-Andrews, 2001, 836). No explanation crops up in the article to explain how their paradigm can be both naturalistic and not naturalistic at the same time. What should the reader conclude?

Whether that vacillation makes sense or nonsense, they believe their investigations support their "predictions" about "infants' perception of emotion expressions" (Montague and Walker-Andrews, 2001, 834). Only evidence-based outcomes count. To their credit, nevertheless, the team admits their study's "drawback; the woman playing peekaboo was a *stranger*" and therefore the infants might have related differently to their own mother, thus yielding different results. Must not 'natural' be a human mother, not a robot?

Change the mother! Well, what else? How about deleting . . . the living infant? Ogino, Ooide, Watanabe and Asada, (2007) allege that they investigate "peekaboo communication" even though 'they' substitute a "baby system" for a live infant. Their design interfaces a researcher (called the "caregiver") with a robot "constructed on a human affect model" (Ogino, Ooide, Watanabe and Asada, 2007, 118). They equip the robot with a camera, a microphone, and a display screen that shows its "facial" images "based upon its *internal* state (Ogino, Ooide, Watanabe and Asada, 2007, 119, my emphasis).

Positivistic experimentation customarily switches both accidental and essential constituents of the game. Even though this experiment played with a machine, not an earthling, it alleges disclosing key structural dynamics of *peekaboo*. Normative conventions shelter it. The researchers defend their conclusion by stating that their findings "correspond" to "observations" and "results" of other researchers that do study live human beings! Does this assertion sound like science or behavior of Club member that use the same codes and play by the same rules? In any event, spontaneous life takes a hike.

The logic of this study, nonetheless, does prompt acceptance that its "sensor data" has spun out information about "the memory module," "the reward prediction module," and the "internal state module." However, an innocent infant does not equate with a robot baptized as a "baby system," nor does a research "stranger" equal the biological mother. Substituting a research assistant for mother, using robots, and so forth studies something, but it is not peekaboo.

"Person-switch": A dubious practice

I found in the literature a more serious issue. Above, I called it unnerving. Should we deceive an infant that is soaking in her earliest and most ordinary impression of the world? In the name of science, is not such deception careless and heartless? It sounds innocent to say, "person-switch" (Parrott and Gleitman, 1989, 291. But listen to how it happens in the living "moment" and how it unfolds. Take infants, ages six, seven, and eight months old. Introduce them to a peekaboo partner. Let them play. That partner hides and quickly comes back, intoning the phrase that names the game. Over trials, the infants come to recognize that person and smile when she reappears. Then the deception comes—the person-switch. The familiar playing-partner hides but a "second adult reappears" instead—to the infant's surprise or shock (Parrott and Gleitman, 1989, 291). Remember that according to Piaget, the infants are at the stage of grappling perceptually-conceptual-emotionally with object constancy. They are vulnerable. Deceiving them demonstrates a lack of awareness, sensitivity, and empathy to the infant's existential-psychological predicament.

The researchers boast about what should shame them: "Infants in all age groups *smiled less following person-switch reappearances than following normal one . . .*" (Parrott and Gleitman, 1989, 291). How do you judge this experimental lie? I wish to be clear: *the deceptive design of person-switch wantonly toys with a young life.*

Rule Structures

Peekaboo, like any game, lends itself readily to a query into rules. Positivistic experimentation handles that task well. In addition, identifying rules fits the democratic-capitalistic ideology of social scientific research, an ideology that prefers restraint, regulation, and control over spontaneity, creativity, or revolution. Research on rules meets with acceptance, financial backing, and an optimal chance for publication.

In 1976, Jerome S. Burner, & V. Sherwood published a seminal study of peekaboo. Three decades of researchers have elaborated or debated the issues it considers. In my assessment, from at the margin, it stands as the most solid piece of work in the entire peekaboo literature. First and foremost, it actually studies peekaboo. Unlike the vast majority of their colleagues, Burner and Sherwood observed live infants and their own mothers at play.

This research team does not experimentally distort or ethically deceive. Reading their article, one sees they do understand peekaboo as peekaboo. However, I pick a bone with them. Instead of using their acumen to study the core fiber of the game, they ape normative rationalism-pragmatism. In what is a mind-game, they assess its rule structure. As Richard Phillips (1967) states, peekaboo has no rules but only requirements. Bruner and Sherwood (1976, 283), however, think they have identified "a set of basic rules":

> Initial contact
> Disappearance
> Reappearance
> Re-established (Author's format).

But those four actions do not constitute "rules." They are simply the 'moments' of the game. Bruner and Sherwood seem to realize the absurdity of their stance: "Peekaboo is a game embedded in *self-directed movement* by the child that produces disappearance and reappearance" (Bruner and Sherwood (1976, 281, my emphasis). Logically and phenomenologically, they might have written next that rules simply do not apply. In fact, they do admit the inadequacy of their formulation:

[P]eekaboo is not a game in the sense of it being governed by rules and conventions that are, in any respect, arbitrary. It is rather exploitation by the mother of very strong, pre-adapted response tendencies in the infant, an exploitation that is rewarded by the child's responsiveness and pleasure" (Bruner and Sherwood, 1976, 283).

If there is as sliver of truth that there is an "eternal conflict between reason and the heart," then Bruner and Sherwood opt for the "rottenness of reason" (Artaud, 1956/1965, 106). Their evidence shows that searching for the rules of peekaboo is a dry and fruitless project. They conclude, however by striking a compromise between rules/no rules, unable to shuck the heavy mantle of the 19th century natural scientific paradigm. Based on our precious western ideological rational dualism, they fall back on a biological cop out by concocting a progression from instinct-to-learned response which turns into "a highly skilled, rule-governed pattern" (Bruner and Sherwood (1976). Pop goes the weasel!

The Bottom Line

The studies I cite above are not communiqués to the common people. They are "love letters" written to other researchers of the same persuasion. The relevance of the research results is limited to those playing the same scientific 'game'. At best, they are irrelevant to daily life persons who want to understand 'what's up' while playing peekaboo, to mothers in particular. T.S. Eliot writes (1936/1963, 161): "Where is the wisdom we have lost in knowledge? / Where is the knowledge we have lost in information?" Both wisdom and knowledge go missing from the peekaboo literature. At worse, the scientists do not even anticipate the potential harm abstract findings might inflict.

What's the bottom line? Peekaboo, as played in homes daily all over the planet and as studied to juggle variables of theoretical models are *not at all related*. A mother plays peekaboo as a natural way to perform her awesome responsibility of **maternal vigilance**. Whereas the scientist feigns neutrality about the outcome of her experiment, mother is fiercely engaged at the level of soul. She watches like a hawk all that is taking place in the game. Like a momma grizzly bear, she protects her vulnerable little one. She earnestly summons everything she can muster within her hearthead to guarantee that nothing will harm her loved one. She would harm whomever or whatever might inflict harm. For her, there is only one outcome of the game: the success of delightful and upbuilding events. She and her infant together will win. Do you have any doubts about which enterprise promotes vitally?

CHAPTER THREE

Hide and Seek

... is an ingenious game. It is particularly brilliant because it cannot fail. Its psychological purpose, in the genuinely soulful, inspired way I have been discussing, is to dissipate the anxiety about being lost. Lost-and-found is a specifically anxious predicament of late childhood, of the juvenile era, of youngsters coming to puberty—kids roughly age five to twelve years. Hide and seek guarantees the security of belonging and safety. If a lad or lassie should become lost, someone will always find him or her.

The prime time to play the game is as the years of enchantment wane but the days of sand and shovels still linger. The kids are no longer "babies." They are "big" now; they go to "real" school and are far too old for soothing parental lullabies. Teacher calls them "boys and girls," not "children"—unless he reprimands them for immature behavior. The sexual awakening at puberty looms, but is experientially far off. Soon it will end one era and open another. After puberty dawns, nobody will play 'hide, go seek' anymore. All the hiding places will be gone then. Gone, too, will be the time for chasing fireflies at twilight. It will be time then for playing with 'real' nighttime fires. But while the mysteries of life remain in abeyance, hide and seek is a favorite game, The game harbors a profound metaphor—and to repeat—forwards the psychological purpose of helping children to cope with a basic anxiety of the preteen age: If I get lost—or foolishly try to hide—somebody will search me out.

In the game, the one who is 'It' stands in the place of the searching parent. It is equally important both that she 'find' some of the children and that some of them elude her and make it 'home free'. To say it one more way, the structure of the game builds in the suspenseful possibility that a youngster will remain lost or undiscovered. But ultimately the searching parent will find her or him. Or the parent will pass her by, giving her an opportunity to dash to the base and find home by her own steam. Everyone experiences a 'homecoming'. The game is fool-proof.

Playing Hide and Seek

"Ready or not, here I come!" That's what the children say while at play. "I'm coming to get you. You can't hide from me! Wherever you are, I'll find ya'! Ready or not, here I come!"

School hours are long gone. The kids have been watching TV, talking on the cell phone, listening to music, or playing video games (most definitely the boys). They have gobbled down their evening meal. Dusk now begins to descend. Perking up, they kill the power of the computer or whatever machine and rush outside to join their neighborhood playmates. Especially the girls will carry with them their cell phones or iPods. Some responsibly have finished their homework: math and science; others race out without even having started their sums, heedless of tomorrow.

The space of the game of hide and seek is far removed from scheduled periods supervised by adults. Play happens with no adult prompting. No echoes harass the kids: "Ok, boys and girls! Log off and shut down your computer. Now it's play-time!" Now they play, not because they have to, but because they want to. At school, they play pretending they are 'playing'. Already as part of their school workday, they have engaged in activities structured by the so-called educational experts. They have dutifully placated the grownups. It's time to play! You can picture the exuberant children can't you? Eager with anticipation, their voices pitched with excitement. "Let's go play hide, n' seek!"

She who is 'It', the one who will do the seeking, places her left hand over her eyes with fingers slightly spread and stands kissing-close to a tree. The kids scatter, seeking a place to hide. She counts out loud from one to twenty: "Eighteen . . . nineteen . . . twenty!" As loud as her little voice will carry, she shouts her warning: "Ready or not, here I come!"

Then she wheels around and begins searching. Her hand, with fingers that had remained slightly spread, slides away from her eyes only half-closed to begin with, eyes that have been furtively peeking while the others scurried, helter-skelter, to find a safe place to hide. In this game she stands for the 'searching' parent. Like Mother Mary in Luke's Gospel she is trying to find the 'lost' twelve-year old boy Jesus in Jerusalem. She is allowed to peek.

A little dancer, she pivots and twirls. On her face a look of breathless wonder, her eyes darting, scanning the darkening horizon, flickering this way and that like spotlights that don't know which way to shine. She giggles, "Where is everybody?" She squeals, "I can't see nuttin." For the sake of the game she must feign half-blindness and pretend that she sees none of the hiding places, pretend that all her children are really 'lost' . . . precisely so she can find them again . . . or that they might 'find themselves' and quickly return 'home.' Remember, it is the essence of the game that no child will ever remain lost and that everyone will experience a 'homecoming.'

Next, the seeker darts swiftly into the gray evening. Her heart beats faster. Objects appear and then swiftly disappear. Abruptly, she halts in order to focus. The stop signals that her little legs had no notion where her run was headed or where she will go next.

In her pause she peers into the twilight's lengthening shadows, glances up at the splinter of an autumn moon. The day has been a scorcher. A "popcorn" storm is brewing. She watches the clouds billow and gather. The pale, anorexic moon is about to be buried behind a dark cloud. Some bats swoop. Fireflies dance around her head like candles in the night. "Lightening bugs, look!" she calls to the invisible hiders. Her arms flail as she tries to catch one, momentarily pulling out of her role in the game. Unseen friendly neighborhood dogs bark like dueling banjos in the darkness, yelping an evening concert of sharp-pitched music appropriate for children engaged in a game of suspense.

The girl resumes her search. She catches sight of the tiny cast of twisting silhouettes, spots profiles of those still trying to hide. Self-consciously, and with anxious uncertainty heads stick out inquisitively, a gesture which asks: "Is she coming?" "Where is she? "I can't see her!" Then they quickly draw back intending to disappear. Other kids are madly dashing this way and that . . . frantically trying to get out of sight and desperately trying to vanish . . . precisely so that they might soon be captured and made safe.

One little girl, Glenna, has crossed the street and has ended up hiding alone in a house under construction. Sitting in the darkness by herself, she suddenly feels scared. Excited and with her heart pounding, she worries that she might wet her pants. She contracts and tries not to budge.

Darla and Allan are hiding together. Hiding together is intimate especially if the two are confined in a space so tight that their bodies are bound to touch. Tonight, these eleven year old kids detached from the rest of the group. Furtively, they press into a space between a large rock, a small Maple tree, and a full bush. While squeezing in, they face each other with bodies flush at the chests in such close proximity that they can smell each other. The scents, like the fireflies that the searching mother just invoked, vividly appear then vanish.

Darla draws back and quickly plops to the ground on a mound of moss. In the act of sitting, her summer cotton dress lifts, curls, and gathers. She leans back on a rock set supine within the earth, trying to snuggle into it. She slightly spreads her legs unaware that her quick descent has exposed her underpants. Allan stares at the tiny patch of white visible in the twilight against the backdrop of her dark tanned thighs. Darla senses more than sees his arm reach and his fingers involuntarily stretch. As she gazes at him she catches his look, his half-open mouth, and watches his transfixed eyes look down at her exposed panties. Quickly, she closes her legs and pulls her dress down over her knees, uttering a barely audible sigh. Allan grunts in response, almost inaudibly. Both look away. A bolt of lightning streaks across the summer sky then thunder rolls. The storm will soon relieve the darnblasted humidity that still plagues the night. In a fleeting interval the boy and girl look back at each other. A flicker of a flame flashes between . . . as they take each other in. Desire then fades as quickly as it flares, like lightening. Allan sits down next to the girl careful not to touch her, making a fist to contain his pilgrim fingers. Darla's tiny hands clutch the hem of her thin cloth . . . shelter. Abruptly both rise and exit from what has ceased to be a haven. She goes to the left and he slithers to the right. As soon as they see the opportunity, both will scoot to the base and the safety of the group. Whenever will this storm finally break?

Meanwhile, the seeking mother stops to catch her breath, catching it in anticipation that, in the gratuity of the chase, soon she will lose it again. She feels a warmth and a vitality as if she were poised on the edge, as if something new and unanticipated was about to happen . . . as if she knew desire was lurking in the underbrush behind a cozy maple tree. Oh, the delicious expectation that the ensuing adventures will take one's breath away, highjack it.

> They prance on winding-paths / meandering towards turning points / trying to enter heaven before 'they' slam the door / looking for the right places of love / chasing lightening bugs /chasing rainbows /following their bliss / imagining far off places /The Northern Lights / The Midnight Sun.

Some "moments" change the course of our lives, "moments" that tumble our world; "moments" we both crave and dread.

Without goals and plans the children flow with the unstructured and unrehearsed action. They shed boundaries and shuck control, bending with the moment and yielding to it . . . as if it were everything . . . as if it were all that ever would be. Oh, my, the incredible serious levity of the "moment" of spontaneous play!

Mother, of course, must ferret out some of the hiding places, smoke out her children from their temporary confinement, and nab a few. When she does seize them, they will squeal with delight. It is so exciting to be found . . . to be lassoed by Mother . . . to feel the warm contact of her hand as she escorts you to the base. Two bodies collide and slightly rub; the touch feels delicious. Like invisible bars mother's arms confine you. Delightfully she is escorting you to shelter, to the comfort-zone of home. One of the little guys she has nabbed, age eight, reaches up and starts kissing her on the cheek and neck. "Stop slobbering me, Henry," the girl complains, starting to tire of this motherly role.

Home base is always ambiguous. Not surprisingly, in some geographical regions the game is called "Prisoner's Base" denoting that one's 'home' potentially holds a double reference. One's presumed haven can also become quicksand, a trap . . . or a jail. Such harsh realities are still at the margin of consciousness of these youngster, just like the sexuality adumbrated in this hand-holding, body contact, and physical escorting is beyond their ken,

As this round of the game winds down Mother has already rounded-up half the crew of players. They sit at the base, on the stone wall that circles the lot. Some hold each other tight. With one or two the touching becomes too familiar. Not satisfied with his attempts at kissing, Henry's dancing fingers are pawing at the breast of Hilda, the German girl who is by far the group's earliest developer. She frowns, scolds him, but draws back and leans forward almost at the same time. These captured inmates patiently await their fate. It gives them license to defy and the chance to take liberties one would never take outside the structure of the game. The game affords spontaneous practice in the act of violation.

[In jail, some men find home, a roof, pillow, three squares, and the possibility of procuring any creature comfort purchasable outside the Wall. Home/prison possibly one and the same thing].

To complete the drama and to extend the game for the night one more event is important. One swift lad should emerge from the dark shadows and race to the base . . . arrive there before the searching Mother can catch him. According to the rules of the game, as he enters the imaginary circle of home near the wall and next to an ancient Oak tree the fleet-footed Outlaw yells, "Re-li-ve-o! I set you free." Or he screams, "Release!" Not surprisingly, in some geographical areas, the game in called by these two words. So the Outlaw (Alapack, 1975) frees the Prisoners. As the children again scatter, their responses cascade: Yahoo! Yippee! We're out!" They screech, "We're free! Away we go! Whee!"

As the gray dusk yields to the light-black cover of night those kids still in hiding now abandon the lonely shadows. Everyone has reached 'home', even Glenna, the loner—who did not pee her pants—and Darla and Allan whose desire visited this twilight like a deliciously fading dream.

The storm has held back but still threatens. So there will be no more scurrying away again "Mother may I"?—also called "How many steps before the King?"—is the 'perfect' next game. This is especially true because it includes an ethical imperative that the loose structure of Hide and Seek lacks. Someone else takes turn at being 'It'. One at a time the players beseech her, the designated "Mother" according to rules. In a pleading voice each in turn asks, "How many steps before the King?"

Mother grants her children to move: "One giant step . . . two baby steps . . . three banana steps." Their little feet go forward advancing toward home base. "Mother may I?" The first child chimes as ritual requires. Once granted permission she scrunches her little body as if winding it up and takes a giant leap.

I saw you move," the Mother tells the second child, the one who neglected to freeze after taking her second baby step. She was trying to steal extra space behind mother's back, mother who may or may not have eyes in the back of her head. "Go back to 'go,'" says the seemingly all-seeing Mother, who in this instance . . . indeed saw.

In a flash, the Mother commands the third child, "You, too, go, back to the base!" In his eagerness to proceed, this boy had neglected to chant the formula "May I?" as the rules that have never been written down demand. He tried to twist his legs forward to make crescent shaped movements in imitation of the large Chiquita banana he had eaten for breakfast. Now he must start anew back from the base . . . so far away from home. He hopes Mother will grant him many, many giant steps. If not he is poised to sprint forward when she isn't looking; this time he expects to get away with it. In the overall sense of the game Mother must see most proper and improper moves so that in fairness she can protect her charges. Mother must also overlook certain transgressions.

Mother doesn't really have eyes in the back of her head, does she?

Darkness falls. The night has become pitch black. Soon the children will be called home. It's a school night. Morning comes early. There's not even time for one more quick game. The kids know it. Nevertheless they extend the game. "One last round," one lad shouts. Not surprisingly it is Henry again. Once the final round begins they will just have to finish it. They will play and play until the exasperated voices of parents start to edge toward anger: "Come home this minute. This is the last time I am going to call you!" In our postmodern age, the cell phone rings: "Where are you? Come home right now! Can't you feel the storm a-coming? It is going to pour down rain any minute now." But the children will push beyond the 'last call.' And push again. Children must defy. It is required.

They are trying ever so hard to grow up.

Before the kids scatter and drift to their own homes and bedrooms all the lines of all the games begin to run together and blur: Kick the can. Duck on the rock. How many steps before the King? Red light: Stop . . . Green light: Go. Yellow light: caution. Red rover, red rover . . . Hide. "Ready or not, here I come." "Can you keep a secret?" "Look before you leap." "Consider carefully before you jump." Stop and go and go until you don't have to stop stopping . . .

The "moment" comes that changes our lives. We totter on the razor's edge, welcoming the miracle in fear and trembling, doomed to choose . . . either/or.

At length some boy other than Henry with a well-aimed voice yells into the ebony darkness, "G'Night! See ya'all t'morrow!" "Sweet dreams," replies reverberate as if from the four-corners of the globe. "Sleep tight . . . Don't let the bedbugs bite!"

You can see them, can't you? Lively children, they play securely and with careless seriousness under a rainbow. Ready in a snap, they are, to leap over the bow of colors; ready to risk. A fleeting "moments" of desire evoke no lingering worries. Its brief appearance easily blends with all of life's realities: with lightening bugs, mangy dogs, and a popcorn storm. These little glad and bold tightrope walkers show no concern about performing without a net. They say to each other with perfect trust, "When I jump, you gotta catch me!" And then shrieking with glee when the "moment" comes: "Now I'm coming! Don'tcha dare drop me! Don'tcha let me fall!"

Blessed be the grownups that allow children to play without interference.

Down has come the curtain on the night. The storm had broken. The rain pelted at first, but now it has softened to a steady stream, to a soft summer rain sounding like a lullaby. It is time to suspend sprints and incantations and true pretending. Now it is time to be tucked in. Now it is time for the candy colored clown to come tippy-toeing into the room. Time it is for the Sandman to sprinkle innocent eyes, clear and bright, with the dust of sleep. All anxieties about being lost and forgotten have been allayed. The balance has been struck between being seen and being overlooked. Permissions have been duly granted and withheld. All the touches, sights, and near-touches have melded together with shrieks of joy and giggles, and with shy and quizzical looks. Now it is time to trust the fall into sleep: to trust that love is stronger than hate; to trust that death, even though It always wins, will be vanquished.

For these children the mysteries of life remain in abeyance. Puberty is imminent even for those for whom it seems to be interminably delayed. We have seen that for one girl and boy it is just . . . a touch away.

For now the children snuggle in with memories of the games of the day returning one more time before they fade into slumber: hop scotch, blind man's bluff and hide, go seek. Tomorrow is another day. New games encroach. Ready or not . . .

"Now I lay me down to sleep. I pray Thee, Lord, my soul to keep."

CHAPTER FOUR

Reflections on Hide and Seek

Double-Bladed Sword

Tension stitches together hide and seek. The game's structure shows two faces. The excitement, secrecy, and intrigue involved in hiding meet and match the diligence, responsibility, and toil required to search and find. A small bunch of players scatter to find a place of concealment; one designated parental figure must hunt them down. The tension of these two actions is, therefore, relational. Imminently, we shall see that the juvenile age is the "actual time for becoming social" (Sullivan, 1953). This preeminently social game resembles an event of dueling banjos; lost-and-found showcases a match of wits.

Tension also punctuates the roles of both hiders and the seeker. In the situation of those hiding, the players scurry about to find a hiding place, thus, staking the claim that they can make scarce if they want to. They act as if they can just drift out of sight of the social other and remain undetected. But the underbelly of the game cradles an opposite meaning. The hiders hope that the social other will guarantee protection, safety, and security.

Negotiating this tension introduces the hiding juvenile to an ongoing social problem that today's geopolitical predicament magnifies. Western democracies have made freedom and protecting privacy primary goals. But nowadays, especially after 9-11, security has become an equal value if not actually our chief one. From the juvenile era onward, individuals must juggle two conflicting values. Even though we enjoy the fruits of the System, it is necessary to challenge the way it erodes our liberty and infringes upon our seclusion and confidentiality. We are watched. A camera focuses on us almost always. Concealment is impossible anymore. Surveillance encroaches on being total. Our sophistication technologies and the Internet have nearly perfected Jeremy Bentham's Panopticon. Visibility is a trap (Foucault, 1975/1979). As the cliché has it, "Big Brother is watching." What price freedom?

The very action of hide and seek manifests two seemingly conflicted tendencies. From the start players pick hiding places that are rather flimsy and easily discovered. They pretend to vanish, but they also let some part of themselves remain exposed to view—an arm sticking out from behind a wall, or a leg dangling from a branch of a tree. In the act of hiding, therefore, they leave blatant clues and clear traces.

The seeker whose job it is to do the hunting and finding…peeks. Although she pretends blindness about the secret places where the brood huddles, the cracks between her fingers and some rubber-necking give her a beat on almost every player. Her feigned ignorance and half-blindness guarantee that her 'charges' will only *almost* be undiscovered but will never be lost. She can zero in on them anytime she wants to. But the game has built-in slippage, too, which allows failure. Mother will pass by hiding spots, as if duped, allowing the fugitives to elude her and sprint to the base. No one goes missing; home remains always in reach.

Trying to find a proper hiding place is part and parcel of the game's adventure. Equally intriguing is 'deciding' with whom to hide. Consciously or less than consciously and in the blink of an eye, each player must pick a partner or two or three to run off with. Natural affinities and already formed friendships co-determine certain pairs or clusters. Some kids, mostly the social isolates, are left out and must fend for themselves. Often they end up hiding alone—like little Glenna in the narrative, scared and isolated in her excitement. Juvenile social comportment shows minimal pretense. It lacks delicacy and sometimes is downright cruel (Sullivan, 1953).

Meaningful accidents also occur during the game. Players arrange their fate or the Universe arranges it for them. The parable describes Allan and Darla, detaching from the rest of the group and gravitating to a closely confined space, and sharing a surprisingly unprecedented "moment" of sensual desire. To use the precise word again, they experience *schaulust*, the lust-in-looking. Allan gazes at her exposed underpants, and Darla sees the look on his face as he gawks. No evidence suggests that they made a deliberate 'choice' to hide together. But a natural and spontaneous logic, deeper than rational or syllogistic logic, holds sway over the encounter. This precise place drew them, did it not? Why not a more spacious spot? Why at this particular time? Why tonight? Why not last evening or tomorrow night? Were they ready for what erupted . . . or . . . not?

Little Henry, rambunctious and precocious though he may be, surely reads well the situation he finds himself in and takes advantage of it. He manifests a keen sense of the situation and does his 'thing'. Henry has learned lessons in the "hobo jungle," namely the social lessons not taught in the classroom or from the pulpit. He sizes up the situation. He steals a kiss and cops a feel.

This tension of the game shows in one more way. Helter-skelter spontaneity, pell-mell actions, and reckless license jostle with rules and collide with regulations. Lawlessness, epitomized by the emergence into the game of the Outlaw, provides the counterpoint to the cardinal needs of the juvenile era: to belong, fit in, be accepted and approved. Horrific for the juvenile is the stings of being ostracized or disparaged. Hide and seek, therefore, also offers a social lesson in the ambiguity of balancing separateness and relatedness, closeness and distance, and spontaneous discipline with inauthentic resignation. What price to belong?

The structure of the game also fosters physical contact and intimate "moments." Mother commonly escorts one of her charges back to the base by holding hands. Or she wraps her arms around her 'prisoner'. The touch is warm. During the escort, stealing extra liberties commonly occurs. Little Henry did it twice.

The erotically tinged "accident" which Darla and Allan share is chock full of meaning. It displays a vivid eruption of desire and also foreshadows sensual touch. The girl's underwear is put to view for the boy. The scene reveals to him an object of desire before he ever desired it. And the "moment" discloses to the girl that she is an object of desire before being one has entered her heart or mind that she might become one. For both the episode adumbrates grownup inter-gender activity. The essence of this juvenile 'stage' is precisely that the youngsters reach, stumble across, or encounter a sensual-sexual object without first desiring it. Sensual-sexual-spiritual desire is present as still "dreaming" (Kierkegaard, 1844/ 1980). By dreaming Kierkegaard means that the juvenile's openness for every impression and attentiveness with wide-awake extroversion makes it difficult in a "moment" to differentiate self from sense-impressions. It is only with puberty, as we shall see, that youngsters clearly distinguish sensation from fantasy. In order to elaborate the point, I pick up the thread of the story in the aftermath of Darla and Allan sharing the awkward experience.

While they try to sleep that night, consciousness presents the memory of the ephemeral "moment" as if it was a dream. Each looks back, gazing through the biblical glass 'darkly'. The sweet secret they share, however, will linger vividly for days on end. The boy will start to stir whenever he re-visualizes the scene of white-cloth-framed-by-dark. He will fantasize seeing what the white covers, and even . . . touching 'it'—whatever 'it' is. Wanting to see and touch what he cannot even picture perplexes him. He jots down in his journal: "It's like being in a fog. Did I see it or make it up? Where did my old body go?" The "moment" of hiding ushers him to a new level in life.

Catching his look promotes the girl to a new level, too. Recalling his stare and her own panicky act of tugging at her dress, she does now what she did not do that night: she blushes. The blush is tale-tell evidence of a secret clashing with modesty. The blush, as we shall see in detail in a latter chapter signifies both embarrassment and pride that she captured his attention so obviously. The blush expresses what is all still too vague to put into words. But in her diary she addresses the adumbration of desire: "My body is brand new now. I feel visible and vulnerable. Did he look at me that way, or did I only imagine it? Anyway, I feel shy and experience strange yearnings fluttering like a butterfly." Sensuous desires flair up, pure and immediate. Both kids are innocent. The advent of desire is dreamlike. Like a sleeping volcano . . .

The Juvenile or Latency Age Child

Who are these youth playing hide and seek? What do five to eleven year old kids look like as a distinct age-group? I will typify the juvenile age, telling you upfront that no youngster of that age actually fits the "typification" (Schutz, 1971, 37ff). I present gross parameters mostly for the purpose of being able to differentiate the juvenile era from adolescence. Between the two eras, a great divide opens. The average eight year old, however just like the average twelve year old or average fourteen year old is everybody and . . . nobody. Do not even once accuse me of giving weight to numbers or to average figures. The bell-curve, both racist and intellectually bankrupt, has no place in this book.

I also describe the youngsters as they behave in the situation of health. Obviously a juvenile in distress or dis-ease shows a very different profile from one in health. By 'in health' I mean more than the mere absence of illness. I describe the juvenile who is at ease with self and at home in the milieu. No one, it goes without saying, is perfectly healthy or so comfortable.

With those qualifications bluntly made, I say that the juvenile age child looks like a sawed-off adult. She or he is a well formed and well put together little unit. The youngster has mastered intellectual symbols. And she or he has sharpened verbal skills such to use "consensually validated speech" as well as most grownups (Sullivan, 1953). The youth in this age-range also enjoys the full coordination of perceptual-motor skills. The sensitive and bright adult can readily "see" those strengths and how they might blossom into adult abilities and occupational pursuits. Visible to the perceptive observer is the budding dancer or athlete, musician or mathematician.

All other things being equal, the juvenile lives the "carefree days." Using qualitative algebra I call them the "days of sand and shovels." The self of the juvenile is enthusiastic. A healthy juvenile shows a zest for life, is interested, oriented, and involved with everything: toys, computer technology, cell phones, TV, cultural heroes, books, the media, politics, church activities, sports, and so forth. The juvenile is a little explorer, searching nature with chemistry sets, microscopes, I-Pods, I-Phones, and the World Wide Web; searching physical nature by exploring caves, climbing trees or mountains, or looking through a telescope. The little unit is open for discovery about the world, and eager to investigate the sea or the lake—whatever is near at hand . . . and whatever is far off.

Erikson (1959) names this orientation and attitude "industry"—the polar opposite of which is "inferiority." Industry carries the connotations of confidence and competence. Open to life and out-reaching, in stance and manner bubbly and adventuresome, the healthy juvenile shows indefatigable energy, dexterity, and skill at what she or he does: skipping rope, playing hop scotch, playing street hockey, or dancing ballet. The youngsters sometimes perform actions with reckless abandon, that is, what appears downright foolhardy to witnessing grownups. The juvenile is often hilarious, too, adept at travesty, burlesque, the comedic, and mimicry of teacher, parent, or TV personality. And she or he is also often a hellion with zest that becomes so pitched as to get on the nerves of impatient grownups.

The juvenile is also a self-starter and initiator. She and he are apt to come home, do homework, and race outdoors to play. Put the accent upon both boys and girls! This is important to highlight because it is too often common practice to try to mellow out the female juvenile, get her to act more 'ladylike'. If not, the tag "tomboy" will be slapped on her. This pressure on girls to tone it down, to soften it, continues into and throughout adolescence—maybe beyond. The so-called "women's liberation movement" did painfully little to dismantle this gender prejudice or any of the other burdens of the Patriarchy.

Latency

Few seminal and decisive thinkers have been more maligned and distorted than Sigmund Freud. In terms of the thinking that holds sway in western culture, especially about love and sexuality, his grasp of the human predicament is too far out of line of the smooth sanitized veneer the rational community prefers. He understands that every part of the human body is sensual-sexual from birth until death and that the flesh is always imbued with psyche. Within that context, he calls the period between roughly ages five to eleven years the calm between two sexual storms (Freud, 1905). The first tempest comes with the Oedipus; the second arrives at puberty.

The sensual flesh, of course, is not latent in the sense of becoming inert or frozen to neutrality. That is not what Freud means by latency. He means that the first storm has subsided. The healthy growing child has negotiated the Oedipus tempest and put to sleep its sexual drama. During latency, emotional-sexual energy of the parental love-triangle and significance abate enough so that the youngster can give self over to reading, writing, arithmetic, to handling the iPod, and diving into the various processes of socialization. Put another way, no new conflicts arise to stir the issues of jealousy and rivalry that beat at the walls of the Oedipus triangle. In a very real sense, the juvenile must psychologically consolidate gains made by the formation of the upper-I or the superego. The emergence of the upper-I, according to Freud is a structural part of the "I" (or Ego) that judges and criticizes itself. A strong enough sense of self put to rest (or represses) the Oedipus complex. Latency is the calm after . . . .

It's a lull not an ending. Whether or not some matter arises that menaces the peace and calm (for instance a parental divorce, sexual abuse), puberty waits in the wings. Puberty lurks. Like the imminent storm that backdrops the hide and seek episode, the thunder and lightning of changes at pubescence adumbrate a new storm to come. The calm before . . . .

In the meanwhile, the 3Rs stare the juvenile in the face. The culture at large demands that the youngster learn and even master impersonal things and processes. Over the millennia every culture expects its young man and young woman to learn its 'technology': hunting, fishing, and farming; cooking, cleaning, weaving, and sewing. Nowadays, formal education is the major gestalt. Not surprisingly, Erikson, armed with his psychosexual outlook, stresses that "industry" is the achievement of this developmental stage. Industry, I repeat, bears the connotations of competence and confidence. The young lad and lass can do things and know new, *im*personal things. One takes pride in what one does well and with one's achievement on the soccer pitch, in the swimming pool, on the dance stage, while winning the spelling bee, or capturing first prize at the Science Fair. Failure to attain the capacity for industry leads to a gnawing and lingering sense of "inferiority."

Harry Stack Sullivan (1953, 117) subsumes the various strands of the juvenile era under one rubric. He calls it "the actual time for becoming social," and he elaborates: "People who bog down in the juvenile era have a very conspicuous disqualification for a comfortable life among their fellows."

Sullivan's detailed elaboration of the various social lessons learned by engagement in the social arena requires a longer discussion than fits the scope of this book. He offers a compelling account the of outlook that human growth happens most importantly as a result of interpersonal provocation / solicitation, not only by biological unfolding, or by intra-psychic consolidation.

The Natural Attitude

The theoretical construct that best subsumes the totality of the juvenile's comportment is Husserl's (1929/1974) the *natural attitude*. School age children-juveniles live in the natural attitude. What does that mean?

Philosophically, the term names our penchant at any age to take things for granted. Things are the way they are and how they appear. We swallow hook, line, and sinker the ideology that our culture propagates. We assume with a simple faith that everything is in its proper place and presume that matters impinge upon us for a reason; or we assume the opposite such that we cling to the painful conviction that the world is a cruel, non-giving place. Growing up in Northeastern Pennsylvania, I used to hear the adults say what communicates simply the meaning of the natural attitude: "You can't fight city hall."

Living in the natural attitude locks the juvenile into a limited perspective. In the apt phrase of Ernst Keen (1975), the juvenile lives as a "satellite" to the parents and the grownup realities of socio-economic class, ethnic views, religious convictions, and so forth. The unspoken convictions are: "I'm just a member of this family, with a certain place within it, within our community, more or less like the rest of my family and members of our reference group." It is a notion that bespeaks narrowness and rigidity. It limits and constricts.

While learning the various 'pictures' presented by those in whom the youngster trusts, she or he typically absorbs the message, repeats it, or acts on it. Listen to any group of ten olds at school, for instance, at the time of a Presidential election. Hear the youngsters passionately mouth the views of parents, grandparents, or select teachers.

The juvenile lives, therefore, largely shaped by forces of the systems within which she or he is embedded. The youngster lacks the keen realization of being a subject who can influence or shape the very forces that shape her. The juvenile is not yet torn by the two-edged sword which cuts both ways and reveals it always can be otherwise. The juvenile has not yet looked at life from both sides. Latency means still seeing life from the innocent side. I would like to emphasize that this innocence is authentic.

The juvenile lives in the natural attitude appropriately. She is still only naturally concerned with a little corner of the world; it is not yet the right time to see the Big Picture. From an ideally healthy standpoint, this time ought to be unencumbered with ambivalence. If the clocks are running correctly, parents and other adult authorities should be taking care of the youngster's recurring and special needs. Without harm resulting, the youngster should be able to walk around in tunnel vision or with built in blinders blocking the broad spectrum of life. A kid ought to be able to trust what parents, teachers, and religious leaders say about the ways of the world and ought to feel good about the ways those grownups act in it. But you and I would have to be wearing rose-colored glasses to believe our kids are so wonderfully sheltered.

Our youngsters need to negotiate what I call the "hobo jungle." The phrase integrates the seemingly unrelated views of Freud, Erikson, and Sullivan. I borrow and bend lines from an old Merle Haggard song about learning things that society's educators never even discuss. Garnering a 'handout' if you are lost, or in a strange town and both hungry and broke is a skill none of our pedantic how-to-do-it books teach, even though it is a matter of survival. Greedy capitalism, which peddles everything for profit, has not yet had the gall to publish *Starvation Prevention for Dummies*. But the Establishment guarantees, by its lack-of-humane policies, that the gap will continue to widen between the filthy rich and the dire poor. Our kids need to negotiate the hobo jungle, therefore, so that their eyes might see through the natural attitude. They must not only fit into the System, but must also change it.

We learn in the hobo jungle by getting involved, mixing it up with and mingling with one's "compeers" (Sullivan, 1953). But it is also learning gained from mulling about and by encountering people and situations beyond one's clan and neighborhood. The hobo jungle is at the margin, maybe a bit over the edge. Coping with what it introduces takes risks. It is learning life from the inside, by getting one's hands dirty, scraping one's knees, and not necessarily keeping one's nose absolutely clean. Adults should shelter such chances for their "charges" to taste raw life and digest it. While getting an education in the hobo jungle, the youth should have as theme song: "Hey, I'm just a kid."

Each of us deserves the chance to be just a kid unencumbered with the duties and responsibilities that will naturally come our way with the passage of time. It is not time yet to question—in the manner of Immanuel Kant—about the conditions that make something possible but not inevitable or necessary. It is not the time to ask about the genesis of meaning in the Husserlian manner, namely that things are co-constituted by the tableau or panorama that confront us and our various registers of consciousness. The juvenile exists within a collective fusion. She is not yet plagued with tortuous questions about the world or doubts about self. The juveniles simply and innocently accept the reality around them. Some youngsters live the attitude more or less dogmatically. In certain circumstances, the adherence to "one's own kind" might be fierce. The injunction "Stick with your own kind" holds power. Walls rise literally and figuratively. To call a spade a spade, fear-spurred prejudice and racism rear their ugly heads. Agents of socialization prefer homogenization and standardization rather than upsetting the apple cart. The major purpose of western education, even more than making money, is revolution prevention.

It is indeed appropriate, even optimal, for the juvenile to live in the natural attitude. The problems of adult life ought *not* to have yet crossed his or her mind. If circumstances do make the youngster question, or provoke doubts, or feel plagued by adult problems, then that youngster has been ushered prematurely into psychological adolescence or even adulthood, no matter what his or her chronological age. If adult issues linger on the youth's mind, then she or he has prematurely been robbed of a carefree world.

Third World kids in particular experience the swindle. Greedy grownups cheat them out of childhood in alarming numbers by forcing them to be child soldiers, child workers-domestics, and child sex slaves. Many less drastic situations disturb and make go up in smoke the carefree days of First World children: divorce and custody disputes; parental drug and alcohol abuse; child abuse, suicide and murder, and the dis-location and upheaval of war and natural and manmade disasters. How long can one be a child in Palestine under Israel's horrific occupation and siege? How long in Haiti where episodic major hurricanes and a monumental (hopefully once ever) earthquake is met with the world's broken promises of help and NATO's concern more with political control than with relief.

Geographical situations also propel the juvenile too soon into adult responsibilities and realities: growing up in our inner cities where crimes of drugs, robbery, and prostitution rule. In terms of our theme, premature introduction to sexuality, especially by sexual abuse, end the juvenile era too soon. The opportunity for a "normal" juvenile experience goes missing. Accelerated into adolescent and adult realities, the youth lack the seasoning of years of dwelling on this planet that help make sense of those realities. They miss out on the daily chance to play those games that ease developmental transitions.

Obviously, by the term normal I am not referring to the ding-dong bell-curve and a statistical norm. Likewise, I reject normal—as typical in mainstream psychological developmental theories—which sets as a standard white, western, middle-class, Christian kids. I take a descriptive standpoint and simply tell of events as they happen and unfold. That which is an 'actuality' for one of us is a 'possibility' for all. My study is color-blind and not biased in terms of creed, class, or status. There is no blue blood either! My heart aches for the Third World kids and inner city American kids who never have the ease to play hide and seek!

CHAPTER FIVE

Playing Tag: First Erotic Touch[1]

Playing 'tag' is as simple yet as profoundly metaphorical a game as imaginable. One kid touches another kid and says, "You're 'it.'" Tag, therefore, copes splendidly with nascent anxieties associated with sensual-sexual touch. It helps to facilitate the transitions between two developmental eras. Kids begin to play tag at the "moment" when the power of lust and the mystery of the other-gendered person enter one's psychic space.

In hide and seek, remember, sensual-sexual-spiritual desire are present as dreaming. One might encounter an erotic object or have a sensual-sexual "moment" before desire emerges. But as the pubescent youngster moves into puberty desire becomes present as "seeking."

The lust dynamism erupts and with it the mystery of the differences between the genders. The budding adolescent lad or lass experiences sensual-sexual phantasies and dreams that bite with anticipation. Nowadays, of course, the Internet flaunts sexuality, floods the screen with soft and hardcore pornography, and supplies vivid images to a teen that stumbles across it. Or another kid or grownup might introduce sexual material to a still naïve girl or boy. But such external images and whatever curiosity they might trigger are merely cognitive realities or sex-in-the-head. Anticipation rooted in one's own desire and imagination, and arousal that comes from one's heart and soul

---

[1]   Playing tag: Gender differences in the transition from preadolescence to adolescence. Presented to *XI th European Conference on Developmental Psychology,* Catholic University, Milano, Italy, 28 August, 2003.

are of a totally different ilk. Desire as seeking is inward. The drive (*trieb*) teamed with the soul (*seele*) spurs sexual anticipation.

Daybreak's rising sun bursts forth with blinding brightness and mounting heat. A new day starts. Something is coming. I await its approach and simultaneously seek it. I ache and yearn for it. It's got me restless. Sometimes, I feel dazed. Dread also creeps up on me. In this 'hour', touch becomes a yen. Emerging lust ushers in the urgent need to touch and be touched back. Touching becomes, henceforth, powerful and important in the lives of us earthlings. It becomes vital to flesh and blood. As my comments about sexual in the preceding chapter make clear, touch can also be used destructively. And our culture, haunted by Puritan attitudes, makes touch taboo. How do we negotiate the first significant sensual-sexual touch? To face this dawn a good game would help.

Teenagers, catapulted to the serious side of life, daily juggle the mysteries of sensuality and romance. It is not surprising that we earthlings have concocted a game to help handle the leap into erotic touch. Tag is as good as it gets. Kids at this age cannot forsake a game that facilitates dealing with the materiality of flesh against flesh and gaining some degree of mastery with it.

The structure of tag, therefore, transitions from ambiguous anticipation to concrete encounter. In the analyses that will follow the parable, I spell out elaborately the coil between the lust dynamism and the mystery of the differences between the genders. Subsequent chapters unveil the more intense and extended clashes between lust and mystery: in the "moment" of blushing, during the kiss, trading a hickey, and sharing a caress. This chapter stands at the beginning. It describes the invasion at puberty. It describes youngsters poised on the barbwire fence between childhood and adulthood. In time, they will jump down from the fence.

Tag is at the beginning. Young lads and lasses, just as they begin to use deodorant, style their hair, and so forth, also begin to change their nightly routines. They put aside childish games. It is no longer appropriate to say, "Mother may I?" or to hide away in secret, or to seek from a surrogate parent answers about the distinctions between false steps and true ones, between dirty and clean, between cheap and expensive, between the expensive and priceless. Henceforth at play, youngsters will leave Mother out of it. Now they prefer a game like tag. For youngsters roughly between the chronological ages of eleven and sixteen, tag is a godsend. Remember, of course, to take all numbers about age with a grain of salt and two or three sprigs of dill weed. Tag might start earlier and definitely lasts into later years. It all depends upon context. What matters here is the same that matters throughout this book: lived time; time that we experience, negotiate, and within which we reach some ending.

Since tag concerns the negotiation of touch, it is also a metaphor for handing the wider spectrum of personal exchanges. In anticipation of what I will treat in a later chapter, touch is one of the richest double meaning words in the English language. When I say, "You touched me," you do not know if I mean you touched me on the outside or on the inside . . . or both. Quality exchanges between people invariably require touch. So tag at an early age jump-starts an interpersonal action that will repeat itself countless times along one's life spiral. And by way of editorializing, if I do not touch you on the inside, perhaps your outside I should refrain from touching.

Let us watch the youngsters play this simple and ingenious game. Watch not as disinterested observers but as implicated and involved. Watch as earnest eyewitnesses who recognize what belongs to us: what we ourselves did long ago; or what our children have done in what seems like just yesterday; or what our grandchildren are now doing. Let us dismantle the hoax of social science: the pretense that what we are looking at has nothing to do with us. If it truly does have nothing to do with us, then why waste time looking? There is so much worth seeing.

"Let's play tag . . . . You're 'it' Get ready! Life, lust, tenderness, and passion are coming . . . and maybe . . . love.

A Playing Tag

"Run! Run as fast as you can, you can't catch me!" The kids are playing tag! Buoyant, brassy, and with daring eagerness they scream the Gingerbread Man's vain boast: "Catch me, if you can!"

The neighborhood klutz is 'It'. He's a slow, clumsy lad christened by the peer group "The White Nerd." The fastest kid on the block is taunting him. This feisty fellow the gang has nicknamed "Mercury." They also call him "Wings." Bending forward at his waist, he teases the nerd: "You can't catch me!" He pedals forward and then springs back, staying on balance and out of reach. Should the Klutz awkwardly lurch, he's ready to pivot and sprint off. Meanwhile, he sticks his fingers in his ears and singsongs with arrogant bravado: "Na-na-na-na-na. You'll never catch me." Winged-Mercury is supremely confident his swift legs will keep him safe. Defiantly untagged will he remain, as long as remaining untouched remains his wish.

Tonight, however, Wings will let the nerd tag him . . . as soon as he can make it look like an accident. At tag, Winged-Mercury never becomes "It." His reputation is at stake. It must appear he was not paying attention. It must seem a fluke not apt to happen again.

A girl is the reason. She is playing, too. Recently, she has sprouted bumps and developed curves. Already, the boys who are dazzled and threatened by her blossoming body have 'tagged' her "The Vestal Virgin." They laugh whenever repeating the phrase. They do not realize they need the incantation to straighten her curves and blunt the power of her sexual physiognomy.

Unbeknownst to her already she has captured fleet-footed Wings. Without trying, she grabs his eye. Whenever she is near, he cannot stop scanning . . . trying to see her. As soon as he spots her, he can't keep his eyes off her. For forever long now, a crazy yen to touch this girl has haunted him. He will not be satisfied tonight until he pursues her, catches her, and deliciously does the deed.

He is not only thrilled that tonight they are playing tag but tickled pink that finally 'It' can happen. Tonight somebody else suggested the game. Last night when he brought it up, the group rejected his request. "You're too fast," one boy remarked. We'll never catch you! It's not fair." But now it's settled. "Tag" is underway.

Soon he will suffer becoming 'It', the pretext for chasing. Under a cloud of diffuse knowing, he can only allow himself to touch the girl under the sanction of the game. If the Klutz should tag him, then he 'has' to chase somebody, right? Why not catch her whose long dark curly hair and pretty ways make him ache?

He feigns carelessness. The nerd nips him and crows, "You're It'. I nicked your arm!" Stunned at his easy success, the nerd forgets to spurt off. But Wings ignores him. The die is cast. The drama starts. The structure of this brilliant game adumbrates what is forthcoming. Imminently, this boy will lay his hand on the first blush of this girl's womanhood. The touch will awaken both. In the lengthening shadows at twilight time, both will experience a new dawn. Then both their worlds will change.

The chase begins. The full moon peeks out from behind a large cumulus cloud. Its bright sheen reveals the swollen appetite on the boy's face. The girl reads the look and grasps that he needs to touch her. The realization perplexes her. Touching her to her seems no big deal. But intuitively she knows it's time to sprint into the unfamiliar erotic darkness.

Neighborhood dogs are barking. A bat swoops. Crickets chirp. The shy moon, female tonight not a man, ducks back behind her cloudy veil. Nature has set the stage. It is starting.

All boundaries are vanishing; girlhood is on the wane. She has known it since she started to bleed. Another betrayal announced it when her body bulged, popped, and sprouted curves. She notices males' "once over" glances; she senses "the second look" as their roving eyes undress her. She blushes a lot now in the presence of the other gender. Although proud of her changes, paradoxically they make her want to hide. Thus, she cannot flaunt them. She wants so badly her new flesh to be perfect, but nobody will tell her how. Sometimes she feels about to explode with vim and vigor; in other moments her soul is as fragile as glass.

With eyes aimed at her, the boy takes his first strides. For the second time in succession, the girl catches the hankering in his eyes. She sees him now as a definite other. In some unreflective way, she knows him. Although this chase will in one sense be typical, it will also be preeminently personal. So the emerging woman within her takes a deep breath. If this chase-and-touch concerns her womanhood, then she will be no passive prey. She is not a fragile flower available for a male's whimsical plucking and not fair game for the male hunter. She can choose. She can scratch him with her fingernails if she wants to, draw blood, or even bite him. Withholding she can flat out refuse, go ice cold, even fake feelings. Or raw and vulnerable she can . . . yield. In this unfolding episode, no matter how fast this star sprinter can run, she will not make it easy for him.

Quickly, he catches up with her adjacent to the Jungle Gym in the school playground. Both stop running at the metal bars. Caught and cornered she stoops over trying to catch her breath. He stands stiff and gazes as she bends at her waist. Her curls dangle as she holds her hurting stomach. He is breathless too, although not from lack of air.

Pleasurable pain cuts him to the quick as he watches her pant. Although the moment is ripe for tagging her, he hesitates. It's only fair that he wait until she bounds back. The group will not think it strange that he does not just nab her. They would figure it's only a matter of time. What has come over him, he understands not at all. As soon as she stops panting, however, he will touch her.

Until now, not counting his mother and two brat sisters, no female has touched him. He is puzzled. Why should he want to touch or be touched by anybody—much less a girl? Why the bursting body of this former scrawny kid? The urge is strong, mysteriously alien, and palpable. He is itching with an itch that he himself cannot scratch . . . an itch, that of all the females who people his private planet, seemingly only she can assuage.

Embodied in this concrete young girl, the ancient but new creature, *Woman* has erupted into his consciousness. In his daydreams, he has pictured peeling her clothing piece by piece, as if plucking a daisy: "She loves me, she loves me not." She disturbs his nights, too. He dreams of walking through a field of breasts hooking his toes on her nipples that appear long and dark like her hair. He is under Life's imperative: to contact her flesh, seemingly so different from his flesh and in its difference . . . numinous.

Extending his arm, his fingers reach so menacingly close that she can feel his warmth. She shrinks back from his reach and leans forward . . . almost at the same time. His fingers are trembling; her legs are shaking. They have come too far to turn back now. Nevertheless, ambiguously cluttered emotions rule the "moment." The trepidation in his twitching fingertips alerts him. He is about to cross a border by touching this female's skin. The only thing clear about the trip over the line is that afterwards nothing will ever be the same. Like all humans at thresholds and in transformative "moments," heightened awareness makes his senses keener. He hesitates. Ache jostles with anticipation and dread.

Touching this Vestal Virgin demands an unprecedented leap. The gun is about to go off starting a new type of race. Afterwards, he will have to find a different way of being fast. Awkwardly, he puts his hands in his pockets for no other reason except that he doesn't know what else to do with them.

In that "moment," she tosses back her locks of hair and expands her lungs. Her chest wonderfully heaves. He gulps. His heart flies into his throat. In a reflexive jerk, he touches his Adam's apple. He fears for his heart. Where will it go next? Is she coaxing it out of him? Is she doing voodoo while he stands absolutely still? What if his heart should next jump into his mouth and then leap to his lips? What would he say? Until now he has only acted boyish around her. However, if his heart should talk what would it betray? He is vulnerable either way, whether she is stealing his heart or if he is about to give it away.

Until now, the rules of the game have structured and sanctioned what has happened. In accordance with them, she should simply submit to his reach. Although trapped at his fingertips, nevertheless she is not ready to yield. Instead she challenges him: "Go ahead, touch me!" Since she no longer struggles for air, her core female self resists. Bitten by anticipation, she uses words to ward off his anxious fingers. At a basic feminine level, she is aware that the only hands that should touch her are ones she desires. "Go ahead. I dare you," she taunts. Simultaneously, she gives him permission and defies. "What are you waiting for? Touch me."

If it were a matter of conscious volition only he would let this moment pass. He would become distracted for an eye-blink so she could scoot off. Then he might feign disinterest as if catching a girl were too easy and start chasing the acknowledged second-fastest kid on the block—or go tag the White Nerd who made him 'It' in the first place. Payback would be reasonable, tit-for-tat.

His Greater Self, however, will not squander the moment, not tonight. Though befuddled about his yearning, he has wanted this night badly. The urgent demand also baffles him that he must touch her and touch her soon. Desire plagues his waking thoughts, his X-rated daydreams, and his toes-filled-with-nipples-wet-dreams. The 'now' is pregnant; the moment is ripe. He must no longer delay.

The scheme of dreams seems so safely distant from the invisible gulf yawning between them. If he lunges at her, what can happen? At best he will span the chasm; at worse her flesh will burn him.

It had seemed so simple. When he started to pursue her it was a piece of cake. Now standing on the edge of this dizzying cliff, poised so near that he can see her perspiration and can smell her, he is reeling. Below this high wire on which he totters there is no shelter of a net.

While he delays she gets her second wind and darts away before he reaches out. She eludes his fingers. He is relieved. He prefers that she glide off. He likes it with his legs under him . . . and moving. He prefers another round of chase.

Still he is much too fast for her. Pursuit is easy. Running to a giant old oak tree she starts bobbing and weaving around it . . . perhaps doing more voodoo. For him it is a perfect moment of rhythmic motion. For her, too, it is the precise pace and place. Now the transaction will not happen in open space witnessed by the eyes of all. The bark of the tree partly will absorb the contact.

Swinging around the Oak his right hand finally touches her. "You're "It" he exclaims. As they circle to the other side of the tree, he grabs her arm with his left hand aware of holding her. Emboldened, he reaches to feel her cheek but touches instead the hair at her temples. Then he trips.

A large root of the oak they are dancing around protrudes from the ground. In testimony to its old age, it is obscure in the twilight. While stumbling, the boy's right hand lands squarely on her breast and his finger catches a button on her blouse. While extricating the digit, he tears off the button and his palm swallows a suddenly exposed curve. For a split-second his fingers grope and then linger on the bare skin. His eyes rivet to a dark nipple. His hand gently squeezes her breast. He warms. She warms, too, in spite of trying to cover her naked breast. The singe lasts only a second. It is the longest second he has ever experienced. Until she will experience her first kiss, never will a second seem so immeasurably long and so incalculably short. Regaining his balance, he moves away from her. Composure is impossible because he had hardened and feels sure that he shows. But he is too shy to try to cover up. She stands staring at him with head cocked and hands on hips.

From a physically short but infinite distance, they face each other. She watches his eyes dart from her face to the hole of her torn blouse and to the autumn moon, still playing peek-a-boo with the stars. His face agonizes. Her heart understands his distress and opens to him. In vague expectation, both kids flicker like living fires that do not know what next to burn. She also wants what he wants but what . . . he does not even know what. She does not know what 'it' is either. Both shudder. She gets goose bumps and switches rapidly from hot unto cold unto hot again. He feels a twinge and a surge, a rising and a pang. Stunned, neither have words. As the awkward moment lingers long, they both blush. He notices her blushing; she notices him blushing. He knows that she knows, and she knows that he knows. Both blush again at the flash of their inter-corporeal awareness. Diffuse sexuality hangs over them, phosphorescent and powerful. How did they just chase away the little kids they were just an eye-blink ago? They will not talk this night except by resorting to ritualistic formulae. Now that the touch has transpired, they will continue playing by the rules of the game.

She tries to touch him back to conjugate this strange touch with another one from her to him . . . to discover if they might generate another spark . . . or if more contact would balance the mighty forces of life and equilibrate the tremble in the Universe. But he will have none of it. Using superior speed to evade her, he dashes off. Renewed play has artificially pumped up his composure. "Catch me, if you can," he yells, almost mocking her. That she is chasing him strokes his unconscious male arrogance. He slows down a smidgeon running just slowly-fast enough so that she can approach him—but not close enough to tag. No more touches will he share this night even though he would prefer nothing more than for her hands to blister his skin. It remains to be seen if he will be granted another night in which such blistering might take place.

For the young lad touching the mysterious other constitutes a triumph of masculine vigor. The victory appeases his urgently stirring tissue tension. His fingers have felt the fragility of a torn button and his hand fondled a warm round vibrating mound. It is enough. He has copped a feel and got some skin. The surface clash, a firm and solid collision, suffices. At last he knows something new and vital. "I felt her," he can say. "I felt 'it." Supremely scary it was, yet so pleasing. He has gone to the dark side of the moon and back. Although he has his first chase and first touch under his belt, his restlessness has not subsided. He is roused more now than ever.

For the young lass this trade is merely a trade-off. The sparks also brought disappointment and alienation. The fleeting hit-and-run touch merely grazed the surface and lacked reciprocity. The hints and clues of a missing button and unprecedented warmth only adumbrate something more substantial, more fulfilling, and more profound to come. Dimly, she senses that someday she will be touched personally, not trifled with, not merely handled, manhandled, and pawed. Her Greater Self recoils at being the passing fancy of a male and an object at the end of his reach. When she taunted him and challenged him for "the more," she had only an adumbration of what that might be. But she desires a gentle caress—although she lacks the seasoning to know the full meaning of that word. This only is sure. She would have preferred to enfold him and that he encircle her. Then she might have experienced a new type of snuggle, and a new cuddle . . . knowing an old familiar warmth plus a new tingle. A fledging woman now because of the chase, she aches for a different jangle and tang. More than a rub and a rip she needs, but rather caresses that linger and last. If she can prevent it she will never have another hit-and-run encounter. She foresees someday being touched all over voluptuously so that she'll fall into swoon. She anticipates what the swift athlete does not even suspect: a touch so splendid that both would never want it to end.

Triumph will come when a man's touch makes her tremble and when her touch makes a man not flee but crave an endless embrace and seek surrender. Bliss will occur when a man strokes her as more precious than diamonds and gold. Fulfillment will be sharing caresses as if there was no tomorrow, as if the world were coming to an end, as if just one special touch might summon a new dawn and create a brand new universe.

She needs such touches to envelop her. He needs to learn that it is possible so wonderfully to wrap. Now it is still beyond his ken. She is standing there staring at him, open, poised and waiting. He is not there yet. He cannot see. He is still running too fast.

CHAPTER SIX

Reflections on Playing Tag

Innocence

The game just described is innocent. It includes no hint of seduction, deception, or manipulation. The boy does not connive or do anything crass. The episode pulls him beyond himself. He takes a risk. As a result, he "earns his spurs," "makes a benchmark," and touches the tip of the iceberg. The experience is nascent conquest and a victory of the mighty forces of life. As the drama ends, however, he is mystified not triumphant. He is still innocent.

When the girl sees on the boy's face his swollen appetite and his ache to touch her, she is—if not shocked and stunned—at least surprised, puzzled, and perplexed. This again, is Freud's *schaulust*, the sexual desire in looking. In the first instance, she is at a loss to know why he is so hell-bent upon touching her! As soon as she dimly grasps the sense of the situation and intuits what is at stake, she becomes neither cynical, nor exploitative, nor seductive. Instead, she draws from her feminine core the strength to challenge the male and summons the moxie to resist him. Nor does she take the easy way out by merely capitulating or resigning herself to the game's rules. Even though she is just finding out that she possess power over the male, she does not take advantage of it. She remains innocent.

The two, therefore, slide smoothly from everyday life with their peers towards the routine and rules of the agreed upon game. Throughout the parable, they manifest a repertoire of behaviors appropriate to the game, as truly as when they were congregating and discussing what game to play. There is no split between life and play.

There is just a shift in intentions. Fluidity hallmarks the differences between the play-situation and what was happening before.

No surprise, therefore, that the entire tag-drama parallels the innocence which holds sway in their respective lives. It is both possible and actual that, in such a game of chase, another girl of the same age and in the same situation would have already been initiated into lust. The game would progress differently. But this girl is unspoiled by prior sexual experiences; and the boy is not calloused by them either. Innocence and wonder mark the action.

Puberty and Beyond: Lust and Mystery

In terms of growing up along the life spiral, what do these young adolescents look like? At puberty the days of sand and shovels yield to the mysteries of life. The newborn adolescent gains new eyes that see a new visual landscape. Now the eyes seize upon the peculiarly sexual. The visible world, corresponding to a new libidinal soul-space, emerges as erotic. D. H. Lawrence (1921/1981, 106)) elaborates: "Now there is new vision in the eyes, new hearing in the ears, new voice in the throat and speech on the lips. Now the song rises, the brain tingles to new thoughts, and the heart craves for new activity." Anything and everything suddenly can and does emerge as a sexual trigger and lure. Funny feelings assault the youngster. Tissues tension is the phrase I use to describe adequately the new and strange fragile, irritable, and excitable adolescent body, the tickling, titillations, and sensual sensation that flair episodically but seemingly randomly, and surely unprovoked. Sexual fantasies also come out of the blue, indiscriminately, at the most inopportune time, and heedless of volition. It is an equally profound transformation for both heterosexually and homosexually oriented individuals.

The Lust Dynamism

Harry Stack Sullivan (1953, 263-296) coins the phrase "lust dynamism" to describe this unprecedented collision with tissue tension, erotic tableaus, with fevered fantasies in day dreams and erotic X-rated night dreams. "Lust," he writes, "is the last to mature of the important integrating tendencies or needs for satisfaction" (Sullivan, 1953, 259). In Maurice Merleau-Ponty's language" (1962, 168-172) sexuality enters existence like an "atmosphere" both as an existential fact and as a permanent possibility.

Don't construe *atmospheric change* as a sheer poetic expression. Instead, remember a time when you experienced such a change. Perhaps you are sitting in a library, restaurant, classroom, or just in a salon getting your haircut. You are gazing off lost in your own thoughts and then someone disturbs your being at home with your self—what Levinas (1961/1969) calls dwelling *chez soi*. Another looks at you, speaks softly, makes a gesture, or touches you. Perhaps you catch her scent. Maybe you get a whiff of the Cuban cigar he has just finished smoking. Suddenly, the atmosphere shifts. The room becomes electrified. It gets hot in your chair. You skin perspires; you get goose bumps. All you can see is light. She is a-glow right before your eyes and you rise. Or he is beaming and your nipples harden.

Sexuality is an *atmosphere* that envelops, animates, and energizes us. It is a warm and bright *field of contact* established between the other and me. Sexuality is an *ambiance* of sparkle and shine, of textures, sounds, and scents. Inside we quiver, enervated and buoyant. We say we are 'hot and bothered' and 'on fire'. Another has attracted us—which literally means has pulled us outside ourselves. All shook up and restless, we *must* move or else we would burst. On the outside, we flush, blotch, or blush. In gender-specific ways we get hard or become like jelly. If pure preference would be granted to us, we would be everywhere and do everything. We would be all hands, all mouth, and all genitals.

Sexuality is essentially relational. Any reduction of it to physiology misses the boat entirely. Sexuality is one way among many by which we relate to one another, touch others, make contact, and break down barriers between us. Lust draws us outside of ourselves. In consequence, barriers vanish and walls fall. "The magic of the dynamism [of sex] rests on otherness" (Lawrence, 1921/1981, 103). Sexuality, therefore, is biology plus.

At puberty our anatomical-physiological body changes. It becomes potent or capable of reproduction. Simultaneously, our lived or experiencing body, the body-subject that co-constitutes meanings also changes. In addition to the physiological abilities to ejaculate, vaginally to bleed and secrete, and to climax sexually, our genitals transform into "zones of interaction" (Sullivan (1953, 282-86). The penis, vagina, and anus alter in meaning. In childhood, they were organs of excretion and elimination only. Along with our eyes, hands and breasts, they undergo a remarkable change and become channels of contact or intercommunicating pipes conducting the flow of sensual-sexual pleasure and erotic satisfaction. They become both flesh-that-desires and "love-zones" (Alapack, 1987). With this new direction and new orientation, concerns unimaginable for the eight year old become paramount: virginity, masturbation, pornography, and homosexuality. The changes affect everything.

> Now new relationships are formed, the old ones retire from their prominence. Now mothers and fathers inevitably give way before masters and mistresses, brothers and sisters yield to friends. This is the period of *Schwarmerei*, of young adoration and of real initial friendships. A child before puberty has playmates. After puberty he has friends and enemies . . . . a whole new field of passionate relationships (Lawrence, 1921/1981, 105)

Lust dynamism accents the maturational achievements and relational changes far better than the over-used and watered-down word, sex. Sullivan, by calling it "the last to mature of integrating tendencies," deletes any pejorative meaning about this radical revolution. He offers a fresh way of looking at the principles and context of growth. Interpersonal provocation or solicitation integrate and lift to a more sophisticated level of both biological maturation and intra-psychic consolidation. Although puberty manifests vitality, an élan and phosphorescence, it also summons excessive enthusiasm and sentimentality bordering on unwholesomeness.

> The child before puberty is quite another thing from the child after puberty. Strange indeed is this new birth, this rising from the sea of childhood into a new being. It is a resurrection which we fear . . . it is the first hour of true individuality . . . It is our most serious hour, perhaps, but we cannot be responsible for it . . . It is the hour of the stranger. Let the stranger now enter the soul (Lawrence, 1921/1981, 105-106).

The Mystery of the Differences between the Genders

Twinborn with the lust dynamism is "the mystery of the differences between the genders" (Alapack, 2007). The fledging adolescent, confronted with the other-gendered person, experiences wonder, awe, and strangeness. The valence of this mystery shifts quickly and with amazing volatility from fascinating to frightening, from alluring and enticing to recoil. Lawrence writes that sex comes upon us "as a terrible thing of suffering and privilege and mystery: a mysterious metamorphosis comes upon us, and a new terrible power given to us, and a new responsibility" (Lawrence, 1921/1981, 113).

We know our own gender from the inside. Insofar as much of the juvenile years are spent having ordinary contacts with same gendered peers, we gain additional familiarity during social activities such as sport, dance, church activities, theatre, scouts, and so forth. Although my chum and I are not necessarily of the same gender, homophilia probably is the most frequent type of first best friend. Through experiences with our chum we learn even about people and relationships more deeply (Sullivan, 1953; Alapack, 2007). We borrow her or his eyes. We learn how to act and interact in what mainstream psychology names, with typical superficiality, "prosocial." ways. In health, an easy peace holds sway.

With the eruption of the lust dynamism, however, everything goes topsy-turvy. A strange creature called "male" or "female" invades our psychic landscape. A radical other faces us and enters into our sphere of relevance apart from any choice. "What is this strange creature called 'female'? "How to I act around boys"? This uncomfortable, awkward, and clumsy unfamiliarity becomes especially strained when gender difference become thematic. Witness "wallflowers" at a junior high school dance, "What does he expect of me? "What does she expect that I expect of her?" "What does she expect that I expect that she expects." At this tender age, furtive glances, and side looks prevail. He looks at her but then look away when she looks like she is about to look at him. This braid of lust and mystery most vividly appears in the "moment" a young girl and boy lock eyes? And the stare evokes a blush. Blushing is the theme of the next chapter.

Structure of Tag

What is the dynamic logic of tag? The young girl and boy are bound for a collision. At the inception of the action, unbeknownst to her, he aches to touch her. Unbeknownst to him are the reasons he is so intending, so impelled, and so driven.

It is a game of pursuing one's desire. At puberty, to repeat, desire-as-seeking becomes more conscious and also focused on an "object." In the parable, the chase searches beyond the obvious—although neither the girl nor the boy comprehends what is the beyond. Salient for the boy is the urge to touch; and for the girl that she has become an object of pursuit. But that is not the whole of it. The drama is about "the more." Neither youngster can anticipate the changes this episode will bring about. The act of touch, the ripped-off button, and the bared nipple are contingent happenings. None of those particulars are essential to the drama. Something else might have happened during the chase. Something inevitably would have happened. What is "the more?"

The first touch is destined to open the proverbial can of worms and the classical Pandora's Box. More precisely, the total situation matters. Context counts. There is no context-less or situation-free first touch. Always it happens within a specific predicament and during a concrete encounter. Each is one-in-a-row and unique. In the parable, the chase is not helter-skelter. It is a subtle dance between the girl and boy. In restless innocence, he focuses upon her as singular object. In wondering innocence, she also notices him as a specific object. Each emerges as a distinct object for the other. They are not just conscious of playing tag but also conscious of each other. A heightened awareness mounts, as the game unfolds.

The emergence of each other as conscious objects for each other co-constitutes the transformative power of the touch. Within the game as described, maybe other players also shared their first touch. But those would mean next to nothing. And if a behavioral researcher questioned to assess how many participants touched the heterosexual other for the first time, the questionnaire would tell us next to nothing . . . no, would reveal nothing at all.

The meaning of the game is the transition from desire as dreaming to desire as seeking. The desiring subject pursues the desired subject. In this drama, the two youngsters are subject-object to both self and to the other. According to Kierkegaard (1844/1980, 77), desire and the desired are one, joined in unity. Hence, a destiny of brand newness comes to pass when the touch takes place precisely in the way it takes place. It is an eye-opener, a heart-warmer, a life-changer. A whole world of anticipation opens. A light flashes in the dark night concerning future man-woman comportment. And the darkness adumbrates adult sexuality. This has happened! Whatever next?

CHAPTER SEVEN

The Blush: An Evanescent Beam of Nascent Sensuality[2]

Part I traces the basic roots of sensual-sexual-spiritual desire. While playing peekaboo in the phase of infancy and childhood, desire is present only in premonition. It is vague, diffuse, and indefinite. During hide and seek, played during the pre-teen school years, desire shows itself as seeking. At puberty and the dawning of adolescence, playing tag manifests desire precisely as desiring. In this section, I describe such acts: the blush, the kiss, the hickey, and the caress.

Blushing symbolizes the early adolescent predicament. A young girl and boy look lock eyes. The awkwardness of the stare broadcasts lust and mystery. At puberty's dawn, the young girls typically receive ravishing glances and feel the stare of being stripped bare. Or guys flash the 'second look' of undressing her with the eyes. Not surprisingly, young adolescents blush a lot, especially in the presence of the other-gendered person. The splendor of seeing is blush-red. *Schaulust,* sexual desire stirred by vision, thoroughly peppers the blush.

---

[2] The Blush: The evanescent beam of nascent sensuality. A phenomenological comparison of sensuality Online and face-to-face interaction. Presented to the Fifth *International Conference Cyperspace,* Masyryk University, Brno, The Czech Republic, 30 November to 1 December, 2007.

The Status of the Blush

Is my reddened skin which makes me look like a tomato just trivial? Trivia in Latin (*tres viae*) means "three ways." Although I tell my online correspondent that she makes me blush, she cannot see my tomato-red cheeks. The blush is only visible face-to-face. The "moment" it flickers between two vulnerable earthlings, therefore, signifies a complicated web of meanings. The blush is complex. It begs for clarification. In what follows, you will decide if it is more serious than mere fluff for poets, novelists, and songwriters.

First and foremost, studying the blush is relevant as a precious phenomenon in its own right. In addition to its inherent worth, the blush also exemplifies an elementary form of erotic life that is visibly apparent to the social other. By taking it seriously, we probe the deepest meanings of flesh as a meld of psyche and skin, of desire and desirability, of the ambiguity of vision and of touch, and even of truth. Yes, truth! As we shall see, the blush not only does not simulate or lie, it saves lives.

Method to Access the Blush: Descriptive Phenomenology

How to capture the blush? Trying to measure or photograph it would make utter nonsense. One must get the story out of the horse's mouth. I collected written descriptions using as stimulus: "Please describe a memorable adolescent experience of blushing in the presence of the other-gendered person." Here come three parables that constitute one way to present my results.

Three Parables

Narrative # 1: About Tammy

It was a classic brother's boyfriend situation. I used to be a little girl only, just the "bratty" kid sister to my older brother's friends . . . until I reached puberty. I remember having a crush on one, whose name was Jim. One Friday night when my brothers were having a party, I sauntered down the stairs feeling particularly pretty. I had just spent quite an impressive amount of time before the mirror, priming and primping—a rather demanding preoccupation in those years. Jim was in the living room, nursing a Pepsi. He looked up as I was making my descent. I caught the look on his face. It was a look of admiration that I'll never forget. With each rotation I made while sashaying down the spiral staircase, he gave me one more "once over." As his gaze roamed from my bare ankles and legs, across my hips, midriff, breasts, and to my face, each gawk looked to me less innocent than the previous one. It seemed his eyes were perusing my every curve, and appreciating the sight with great relish. Surprisingly, I easily read the looks: "Wow! This is a woman! I can't keep my eyes off. She attracts me." When I reached the bottom of the stairs, he stared at my cleavage for what seemed forever. I was wearing a provocative V-neck tight black sweater. The thought flashed, "He is trying to look through my clothes. He is undressing me with his eyes." When he gazed directly at my face, I felt naked. That's when I lowered my eyes and blushed profusely.

Nothing was said for quite a few moments. Time stood still in eternity . . . as if applauding my new found power over men. I was tingling inside and feeling hot and sizzling. I had changed into a living neon light bulb, glowing from my scarlet cheeks right down to the tips of my naked, painted toes. The fact of being observed in this manner awakened in me a newfound femininity, an insatiable need to be noticed, and secretly desired by the opposite sex. Dimly, I sensed a potential for some new meeting, one which I knew nothing about but which excited me to no end. It was not a lustful episode, but an awakening to a newfound urges and drives that I knew nothing about. I did know our relationship would never be the same after this. If he had blushed too, I didn't see it. But he looked nervous and restless. From now on, I would be treated with respect by the older boys and regarded as a female that triggered chemical attraction which could no longer be ignored.

The experience made me proud of my newfound physique. It was difficult being the first girl in the family with two older brothers. No one had gone before me to pave the path to adulthood.

My budding breasts and shapely hips were something of which to be ashamed in my family. My family expressed no excitement for my recent changes, much less said anything to flatter me. My father would look at me out of the corner of his eye, in dread; my mother watched with equal trepidation. My brothers, however, gave little acknowledgement, seemingly ignorant of my recent allure. Even my little sister appeared dismayed that we no longer had baths together, and disgusted that now I had glorious form and hair in places where she did not. She was trying to hold onto the Tammy she knew; but that Tammy no longer existed, either in body or in spirit. The Tammy of naive innocence and splendid unpretentiousness could never return. Suddenly, I knew she was gone forever. But secretly I smiled inside. Watch out world!

Narrative # 2: About Paul

We had just taken a nice long walk on the Santa Monica beach. Tentatively holding each other's hands, we had talked and talked and talked. It was dark, so it was hard to see each other. But we could feel the tension in our hearts, our voices, and in the grateful grasp of our sweaty palms.

This is the picture I would paint. I'm not sure it's necessary. The important part happened when I dropped Charlotte off back at her house and saw her standing in the light.

God, it's like I remember but don't remember at the same time. How long did we stand there? It was a year and an instant. Her eyes really looked at me. For once, I didn't look away. I saw a lot in them in that moment that provoked a blush. "This is supposed to happen only to teenagers," I thought. "Here I am a late developer of twenty-three." The blush was heat, stifling but refreshing. I wanted to gasp for air, but simultaneously not breathe at all. I realized that she really likes me as me. I didn't need to say a word. I only had to be there.

The question flashed, "Would she blush too?" She did. It must have been the air between us. Seeing my blush made her blush, too. We became extremely self-conscious but, in a single moment, also acutely conscious of each other. In a flash, I was thrown back years. I felt 16 years old for the first time. When I was sixteen, I never felt like that. I wanted to get closer to her. She was standing two feet away, but I felt like I couldn't move. I wanted to speak, but I felt like it would ruin everything. I wanted to touch her, and knew that she could be touched. All my doubts and insecurities rattled like old bones inside a box, dusty and harmless. This was the beginning of something new and strange. I had desired such a feeling for years. But I could never just manufacture it. How could I ever have envisioned feeling so ecstatic and uncomfortable at the same time? We kissed. I don't know how I got home.

This moment was not only my most memorable blush, but it was also my first realization of myself as a sexual being. Having not dated too much in high school or very steadily in college, I experienced a moment of truth. I was confronted with the fact that I'm not in control. By my blush somehow I'd given something of myself away that I didn't even know I had. It was a complete surprise. And in retrospect, it has continued to surprise me. I'm surprised I remember it so vividly. I'm surprised I still feel it now. Was this first blush also the moment I realized my first love? I still wonder what was in her eyes that night. What all did she feel? Whatever did she realize or not know? I wonder about it like a mystery that tells one so much but remains a mystery.

Narrative # 3: Not yet Lingerie

I had known Ron for a long time, for five of my twelve years. Every summer, my family came to the lake. Every summer, he also came. And how I adored him! He and my father were very close friends. I loved to hear the rumble of their deep voices as they discussed and shared views on religion, education, politics, and other manly topics. But he was my friend too, exactly ten years my senior. It was our huge joke, our special sign, that our birthdays were exactly one day and one decade apart. Ron was the older brother I longed for. But he was even better than an older brother because he never teased me cruelly (just happy, eye-sparkling jesting), or yelled at me, or called me insensitive names, or wished aloud for my immediate demise. During our summers together, he took me fishing; he taught me to swim, to row a boat, to play shuffleboard. He identified poison ivy to me on one of our companionable hikes; he ruffled my hair: he swung me around with his tanned arms under my armpits and wrapped me across his chest. He nicknamed me, from the novel *Green Mansions*, "Rima, the Bird Girl" because of the way I would fly around his body. During the winters, I wrote him long letters to his college campus in Indiana. I always began my missile with an atrocious juvenile joke. He always came over during the Christmas break, when he was home for the holidays. His summer tan was faded, but not my adoration.

In early July, when I was 12 years old and just beginning to feel tingles of sexual pleasure, I eagerly awaited his arrival and rushed madly to his cottage when I knew he was there. Following my custom I flung open the door, ran into his bedroom, and plopped on his bed. But my joyous greeting stuck in my throat as I realized that my sundress had flipped up, curled, and my underwear was showing, Ron was watching me as I looked up, struggling off his mattress, and pulling down my skirt. I had never seen a look on his face like that before. A brilliant crimson, hot blush crept over my face when our eyes met. Suddenly, I felt that he could see all of me, that he was looking right through me. His eyes seemed riveted to my face. That made my warm cheeks even warmer and made me blush even more profusely. My underpants! Oh, how shameful.

CHAPTER EIGHT

Reflections on the Blush

The Significance of the Blush: A Leap

What does the blush signify? Sexuality has entered existence like an 'atmosphere' (Merleau-Ponty, 1962, 168). One is aware both of erotic ideas and possibilities and that another knows of your awareness. It is emotionally tinged shared knowledge. Last month, last week or even yesterday, the same boy might have leered at Tammy in the first narrative in the same invasive way. She did not understand the look then. She looked right through it. It meant nothing to her. Now she understands his stare and her skin feels it. It warms her; she blushes. In an eye-blink, she has reached a new personal level. Kierkegaard's (1843/1971, 335) description fits her, "A young girl does not grow, she is born . . . . She does not awaken by degrees, but all at once." Prior conditions cannot account for this change. It is not an additive process. It does not happen as a result of one more day, or experience, or event that completes a series. It is a leap. A young boy crosses a threshold with steps. A young woman reaches a new level in one fell swoop.

What does it take to blush? What are the necessary conditions? Skin is imperative. Blushing demands the flesh. It requires that we both have and are a body. If there would be angels, they would lack a body and could not blush. Our most recognizable and loveable droids, R2D2 and C3PO, do not blush. Nor does our precious pet extra-terrestrial, ET, blush. It is an open question whether Jamie Sommers, the Bionic woman, or Wonder Woman, whom we will consider in a later chapter, blush. Flesh, blood, and bone are necessary.

Secondly, blushing also requires sure but ambiguous consciousness of my body as visible, sensual, and erotic. Such awareness is spirit in the sense of the French *l'esprit* and the German *geist*. Human bodies are both physical and spiritual. Spirit signifies that I have a relationship with the realities of my life. I do not only work, play, pray, and love, but I also relate to my life, my death, my sexuality, and my bliss. The spirit, writes Nietzsche (1889/1982) is "life itself cutting into life."

Thirdly, the blush necessitates a complex social membrane: an intercorporeity and shared consciousness which connect us to an erotic field. "Nobody blushes alone," Lingis writes, "To be troubled erotically is to be concerned about someone" (1983, 63). The blush is a phenomenon of my shared world (*mitwelt*) (Binswagner, 1944/1958, 337). I do not blush in the dark, no matter what I might be thinking, feeling, or doing. Blushing demands a simple yet complex inter-consciousness: You-know-that-I-know-that-you-know; I-know-that-you-know; we-both-know ... about our sexual situation.

The Stare

Jean-Paul Sartre's (1943/1966, 340-400) peerless phenomenological description of the "stare" captures in a nutshell what is at stake. Sartre posits someone at a door, leaning over and peeking through the keyhole. He never says what is behind the door. He just relates that I, as onlooker, survey the scene as pure, unfettered consciousness with no check on my spontaneity or freedom. But then, I sense that someone has turned the corner. I peer over my shoulder and see that someone is looking at me. That look, Sartre says, steals my world. In a flash, I have turned into an object at the end of the other's look. Consciousness finds itself totally unjustified. It is the moment of shame. Unexpectedness is part and parcel of the "moment of embarrassment." I am caught by surprise, unexpectedly exposed, caught red-handed, metaphorically caught with my pants down. I blush.

J. H. van den Berg (1972, 70-71) goes to school on Sartre. He describes the blush as a "barrier of blood" that both hides and broadcasts fledgling sexual desire. One recoils at being gazed upon as a sexual object, while simultaneously one wants to inhabit the desired eroticized flesh. The blush signifies primary "existential shame."

Levinas pens, arguably, the loveliest line in all western philosophy, one that I use as a chant throughout this book: "The eyes do not shine, they speak" (1961/1969). In terms of our theme of sensuality-sexuality, the gaze is critical in co-creating the way we live our identity as a man or woman. The voluptuous eye is on the lookout for the alien look, and wants to be the look that the eye of the other seeks (Lingis 1983, 13-14). Quite normally, such looks institute schemes that orient my vision and my bodily action. Do we not learn to focus our gaze by reading the way that others look at us? In the context of the blush, the vacillating adolescent is on the lookout for the glance of the other, for "knowing looks" that seems to interpret one's tender soul.

The eyes do not shine, they speak. Traditionally, the eyes have been considered the window to the soul. Visual artists, actors, and directors of stage and silver screen are ultra-sophisticated about the way a glance, a smile, downcast eyes, or a far-away look can carry the sense of a scene or determine the portrait. But our educational, psychological, and medical literature overlooks this vital link to relevant knowledge of everyday life. Mainstream social scientists and behavioral technologists are ultra-naïve about such splendid realities, and even ultra-naïve about why such matters . . . matter.

It suits to clarify the meaning of this existential shame, the power of the eyes, and the warming of the blood. The kernel idea is that I am an embodied self, psyche-in-flesh, not a duality. Suddenly and unexpectedly, my whole self falls under the gaze of another. I am exposed. The situation draws my nascent sexuality to the foreground of my awareness. But for whatever reason, I am not at home with my Self as a sexual being in the situation at hand. It could be that it is the wrong person, or the wrong time. In my narratives, it is a matter of the youngsters not having reached certain developmental milestones. To use the five dollar word, sexual thoughts and feeling, especially in a public context, are non-ego-syntonic. Tammy, Rima, and Paul have not appropriated yet their burgeoning sexuality. It has not become comfortably "mine" to them. The other looks at them in a way for which they are not ready. To that extent, they feel unjustified, and they blush.

Tammy notices Jim undressing her with his eyes, appreciating her newly developed breast and curves. In a flash, she "reads" the sexual glance and it changes her. Her innocence wanes as the distance between her greater self and her lived body is simultaneously enlarged and minimized. She blushes because the look carries her beyond being the little girl body that she was looking at in her bedroom mirror just minutes ago. Under Jim's appraising gaze, it has changed into a woman's body. The blush signifies the ambiguous relationship between desire and desirability. There is no distance between her embodied self and his ravishing stare.

When Tammy blushes, she becomes more visible than she was before she "caught" the boy's glances. She does not know if the young man can read her mind, or read her heart; but he surely can read her blushing face. So, she knows and she knows that he knows.

It is similar with "Rima, the Bird Girl" in the third narrative. Ron's eyes co-constitute the blush. Ron is staring at her suddenly and accidently exposed undies. She has become visible to him in a new and unprecedented way. Fully clothed, she is nonetheless caught without having on all her feathers. There is no place to hide. She, too, is more visible after she blushes. "How I adored him!"

For Tammy and Rima nothing will ever be the same. It is a 'moment' of transformation and of transition. We cannot measure it. We do not have to. We can see it. It happens right in front of our eyes.

After their long walk on the beach, Paul and Charlotte are standing face to face, taking forever to say "good night." Their eyes lock. He blushes first. Then she blushes. And they both blush again. By blushing about blushing, they become more acutely self-conscious, more conscious of each other, and more visible to each other. Graced by the splendor of seeing, they seize the 'moment', risk the magic of touch. They kiss.

What is happening? In each situation, blood goes out to meet the looks. The blush creates a blood-barrier behind which the youngsters both hide in innocence and shine forth in newness. Blushing marks both a lack of at-home ness with erotic flesh and a budding intimacy with it.

When they will grow older, our two young ladies will choose to inhabit fully the sexual body. It will not be a 'moment' of surprise. Without a demure distance from the flesh, they will drop the barrier. They will peel their clothes, proud of flesh that does not then and there need cover. In the "moment"' each chooses to become a woman entirely, no blush will beam.

The Language of the Heart

I call the blush a life-saver. James Lynch (1985), a world-class cardiologist, has marshaled compelling physiological evidence that support my analyses. The cardiovascular system is at stake. There is a link between blood-flow and the response of blushing. There exists between a man and a woman "a tremendous magnetic urge towards the blood" of the other (Lawrence, 1921/1981, 106). Lynch affirms an even less obvious connection, "the hidden dialogue" between the objective heart (a pump for circulating), and the living heart (a subject of experience and feelings). He demonstrates that an adequate understanding of the human heart requires that we see it at three interconnected and interactive dimensions: a biological objectified pump, an organ of communication, and a subject of human experience. If your physician ignores the latter two dimensions, she is functioning ethically as a trained medical doctor, perhaps, but she is not dealing with the human heart. She is only dealing with a scientific abstraction.

Lynch is clear. Blushing is an interpersonal experience. An essential part of blushing is its public visibility. "When two human beings speak to each other," Lynch (1985, 206) writes, "their bodies are also simultaneously engaged in an astonishingly complex dialogue .... human beings have remarkable power ... of transactional forces over each other's bodies." The transaction expresses unequivocally a link between my body, my emotions, and the social membrane. Furthermore, the link is transparent. The face broadcasts spontaneous emotions easily decipherable for the observer and simple for the individual to acknowledge and own. The blush, therefore, does not simulate. The anatomical-physiological heart tells the truth about this ambiguous "moment." In whatever variation the question is posed, it always means: "Are you embarrassed?" The equally honest answer is always, "Yes, I have feelings that I would like to deny but cannot hide." If the blusher should equivocate in response, the questioner would roll her eyes and stifle a sigh of disdain. The reddened face has already demonstrated truth-in-the-flesh. Blushing, therefore, saves the life of the individual by bringing emotions out into the open. Repressing strong emotions over time contributes to essential hypertension and may lead to an early grave.

Lynch underscores that we must not ignore the blush because it protects the integrity of the cardiovascular system and also ameliorates emotional isolation. As a shared human experience "blushing is an interpersonal vascular signal and important bodily message. It interrupts all ongoing dialogue and demands a response" (Lynch 1985, 208-209). It supports health. He articulates the psycho-physiological key to the blush:

> Since blushing involves the social membrane, it connects other people to our distress. It leads us to see ourselves and to feel our embarrassment through another person's eyes. It forces us to think about and to feel what others are thinking and feeling about us. It establishes our sense of self in reference to others (Lynch 1985, 209).

No Simulation

Whenever I say that blush always reveals the truth, my philosopher friends correct me. They are right from one perspective. It is not truth in the classical philosophical sense which defines truth as correspondence between "reality" and my idea of it. The blush reveals truth in the sense of unveiling, uncovering, or disclosure. Something comes to pass. It comes to presence from hiding, lingers awhile, then recedes, and something replaces it. Truth is not a static meshing of two contrived dualities of mater and form, or of the real and ideal. Truth emerges within the movement of Life's flow and of human action.

The mercurial flash of the blush, so vividly noticeable and comprehensible, tells the truth as a reliable existential guide to living with others, moment-to-moment . . . in matters of the heart. Nietzsche (1885/1955, 87) writes, "We may lie with our lips, but we tell the truth with the face we make when we tell the lie."

The blush, therefore, is an existential diagnostic tool. It detects immediately, naturally, and spontaneously an individual's vulnerability with no hypothetical translation or reconstruction necessary. The onlooker automatically and unerringly sizes up the blusher as someone not cold, calloused, and calculating about whatever matter has provoked the beet-red cheeks. The bona fide criminal thinker, who lacks the feelings of shame, guilt, regret, remorse, does not blush. It is another matter, of course, to decipher the core of the vulnerability. Our interpretation is never a led pipe cinch. Is it a blush of embarrassment or shame? Is it about sexual desire or loss of face? The exegesis takes labor, of course. But it is an ordinary human process.

"Man is the only animal that blushes, or who needs to."

CHAPTER NINE

The Adolescent First Kiss:
Our Gateway to Romance[3]

Like a colossal knot, the kiss is woven in variegated strands throughout the history of human love. Arguably the story of the kiss mirrors the whole tale of human affection (Perella, 1960, p.10). Kisses punctuate our own tales of romance, both memorable ones a perhaps few botched attempts.

To tell the story of the erotic kiss, I start at the beginning. I start with the adolescent first kiss (Alapack, 1986; 1991a; 1991b; 1993; 2001; 2006; 2007). The next chapter considers kissing in general.

Our first kiss, in whatever the circumstances it happened, was a revelation. To enter most personally and fruitfully into this chapter please recall your own first kiss. Also conjure up your own list of romantic-erotic partners. Reflect upon *the place that kissing held within your relationships*. Here comes an exhaustive report of my qualitative research on our gateway to romance.

The Adolescent First Kiss

Who cannot remember the time when whether to give or receive our first real kiss was a living question? Many of us waited with longing that first touch of another's lips. Others dreaded it with

---

[3]   Adolescent first kiss. Presented to the *Fifth International Human Science Research Conference*, the University of California, Berkely, CA, May 1986

an all-consuming irrational fear. Still others found ourselves precipitously plunged into the heretofore strange situation. Some of us do not remember it at all. How did we negotiate that unprecedented moment wherever it happened, or whatever our age, or whether we were eager, overwhelmed, agonized, graced or stunned? Our respective stories of initiation into kissing are uniquely precious. Like tales of the blush and the hickey they are not only cutely trivial material for poets, storytellers, and songwriters. The kiss is a significant phenomenon in its own right and should be leveled down to a beginning sexual activity, a form of foreplay, a step toward genital intercourse, a warm-up for the main event, or the appetizer before gourmet lovemaking.

First Fore-sense: Ambiguous Anticipation

An adolescent inexperienced in the "subtle and delicate art of kissing" awaits the first touch of lips with both eager enthusiasm and worrisome dread. The kiss appears as both an "insurmountable threshold," an "important hurdle," or "'barrier'" on the road to becoming an adult. It also seems a baptism under fire," a "true test under game conditions," or "a trial by whichever might burn the most . . . acid or flame."

The still unrealized moment, poignantly desired, is a cutting edge. Expressions that qualify it include: interminable, in restless wonder, nerve wracking, or a wistful longing for what seems like it will never arrive. The waiting adolescent worries and plans, plots and schemes, daydreams and frets about it. Antinomies hold sway. One is equally convinced that the kiss will take place with mysterious rapture and yet terribly sure that it will never happen. Likewise one is supremely pleased to be waiting for the right partner to come along, yet enviously certain that all one's friends have already enjoyed the sweet taste of that first lip contact. Reveries about the scene of the possible kiss are polar too: either romantically perfect in sight and sound—knights in shining armor, Technicolor heroes, cascading waterfalls, enchanting, music, pealing bells—or perfectly horrible in dizzy vagueness and total unfamiliarity.

Anticipation is equally conspicuously meaningful by its absence. We shall see below that awkward and alienating consequences follow being kissed without having first experienced the bite of expectation.

Agonizing Questions/Fantasies

Layer after layer of increasingly difficult and eternally awkward questions plague the still un-kissed adolescent. In light of the big build-up about it, they are supremely serious. The basic questions of whether or not to kiss and of whom to kiss dovetail. The situation is even more complicated since all imagined answers appear with equally frightening consequences. If the young man should muster the nerve to make the major move he wonders whether his heart throb will turn away in rejection, submit passively, or actually return his kiss. "Will she duck or deftly fend me off by a perfectly timed turn of the cheek?" "Does she expect to be kissed and think I'm gay if I don't try? If I take it for granted to try will she think I'm a presumptuous jerk?" "Should I assume that I can kiss her, or will I shock and scare her by swooping in?" "How can I ask without sounding like I'm getting permission from my mother?"

The young woman wonders if the guy will find her desirable. But if he should try to kiss her, she is equally concerned about his response to her behavior. "If I chicken out, will he ever ask me out again?" "Will he think I'm frigid if I refuse?" "If I steal the initiative, might he judge me a cheap sleaze?" "What will I do if he tries to 'deep kiss' me or wants to pet?" "Mother says guys only want 'one thing'. Does he think a kiss is first base, a brief stop on his way to an inside-of—the-park home run?" However the girl acts, she wonders if he would put up a poster at school next day proclaiming it and worries what stories he might tell his pals in the locker room. A male compresses many typical questions into a short lyric about the kiss: "Lose it, steal it, keep it, bestow it . . . blessing or burden?"

The Art of Kissing

Once the inexperienced youth decides to risk kissing matters are not settled. One is merely beset with new quandaries. One lad writes: "I was studying French in school. I learned about 'savoir faire'. I knew I lacked it." The following sections show that the issues of technique, mechanics, or strategy pervade the entire kissing predicament.

The Eyes: Open or Closed. "If I close my eyes, will I miss, hit her shoulder, or get a face full of styling gel? But it might be eyeball to eyeball if we both keep our eyes open." "I kept trying to visualize the way I saw it done in the movies. I would have been mortified if I closed my eyes and we bumped heads." "What if I closed my eyes and our lips missed, or only almost met, creating a ridiculous half on half off variety?" A male says: "Bending over I closed my eyes so soon it was a wonder I didn't kiss her of her chin. Fortunately I hit the right spot only to find, in horror, that her mouth was open." Or one girl worries about her specs: "How does one execute a kiss with eyeglasses on?"

The Mouth and Lips. Oral concerns are salient. "The fear of halitosis creeps over you like a dreaded disease." What is the right mouth-pressure to exert? What degree of wetness distinguishes sloppy from moist? Teenagers worry about a tooth clash. Especially those wearing braces fear an embarrassing visit to the orthodontist's office. "If the miracle happened, was it going to be with his mouth closed or an erotic 'soul' kiss? How was I going to accommodate his open mouth expecting a 'French' while mine was closed (or vice versa)? I came to the brilliant deduction to have my mouth semi-opened, ready for anything." Another female writes:

> Finally it hit: the invasion of Normandy was relived. There was a war inside my mouth. This was not liberation. I had properly closed my eyes and offered my lips when he placed his hands on my shoulder. I had in my romantic naïveté anticipated a gentle kiss on the lips. Instead he pried them open somehow and

invaded my mouth with what felt1ike his whole face. I was later relieved to discern it was only his tongue.

The Place of the Face

You start to lean in and then you develop the "big face syndrome" with your face feeling like a huge and misshapen Goodyear blimp." "Our lips met. He opened his mouth and tilted his head to the right. I closed mine and tilted my head to the left Oh God, how could I do that! The only things that came into contact were our noses." "Where do the noses go" also typically perplexes those still not kissed (Hemingway, 1940/1968, 71). Sartre (1948/1976, 197) describes an allied concern: "He wanted the kiss to be long and successful but he wondered how people breathed. Finally, it was not as difficult as he thought; it was enough to kiss on an angle, leaving the nostrils clear."

The Role of the Arms and the Hands

"We started to move towards each other. I didn't know what to do with my arms. They seemed to be dangling like two elephant's trunks. I tried to picture how the guys in the movies and on MTV wrapped their arms around the woman while kissing. And I didn't have a clue what the hell to do with my hands." "Spontaneously, I put my arms around her and started to pucker as our lips seemed close. My right hand was around her waist. Suddenly, my fingers felt flesh. She was wearing those low riding jeans. Her skin felt smooth as silk and warm. Instantly, I got a raging hard on."

Duration of the Kiss

How long should the kiss last? "If it lingers too long," one guy mused, "will she think I'm after sex? But if it's just a quick peck she might think I'm an inexperienced nerd." "If it's too short," a female pondered, "will he think I'm a 'cockteaser'? But if I prolong he might consider me a 'slut'. What's a girl to do?"

If one stops the kiss too soon, there is no way to return gracefully. One fellow, reflecting humorously upon the "catch-22" nature of the situation, insists that "the average length of the first kiss is fifteen seconds or eternity . . . whichever comes last."

The Space of the Kiss

The neophyte agonizes about the preferred place to kiss, either the private, convenient, or romantically perfect spot. "I prefer to kiss people without witnesses," says Maugham's (1919/1982) youthful protagonist. The ambiguous relationship between measurable space and personal, lived space confounds one's priorities about the right spot. Typical places where first kisses are most frequently realized and equally frequently avoided include the front porch, the driveway, the living room, the family room, the dark corner, or the 'make out' room. These are not just geographical sites. According to the total context, each spot is imbued with meanings peculiar to each partner. Contrasting views about the suitability of a particular setting for kissing co-create complicated happenings.

Politics of the Porch

"Walking down the driveway to her front porch was like a two-step. Walk halfway up, stop, talk for a while, walk a few more steps, crack a joke, inch a few steps closer to the porch." For this male, negotiating the driveway is his 'longest walk'. Finally reaching the front porch is like 'conquering a beachhead' or arriving at the 'threshold of paradise'. "I couldn't believe that I was actually standing at her front door! It seemed natural to put my arms around her and kiss her good night." But no! To her it's a short driveway, familiar turf she has trodden a thousand times. But can she kiss there? Not easily if she feels like she is under a microscope awaiting her parent's intrusive flashing of the porch light. Not smoothly if, while standing at her front door, she feels watched from behind a one-way minor. And so they let the opportunity pass.

Another female relates: "He walked me home. We stood on the front porch of my house. We could be seen for a least a square mile in every direction because my parents kept the porch light on whenever I was out on a date." The lighted porch, intended as a deterrent, bothered her not at all. "I didn't share my parents' idea of feminine modesty." But the boy was not ready for her readiness to kiss, since he felt under the light like he was 'on candid camera'.

She 'knows' it is perfectly safe to kiss in her family room since her parents are at a party and her older sister has promised to keep herself conveniently scarce. But he feels no affinity for the surroundings and is too vigilant to relax. "My ears were like radar—alert to any sign of motion elsewhere in the house. Her eyes were closed as though she was off in a dream. Mine were wide open and peering over her shoulder in case someone came down the hall."

On their third date, he takes her to his favorite place on earth. They walk to the beach, dazzled by the "'June sun glowing off the horizon." Lying on the sand counting the stars, he is in his element and aware of a certain 'magic' in the night. But the beach is not homey to her. She feels the absence of privacy "as if the night really had a thousand eyes."

The same setting, sufficiently safe, private, or intimate to one adolescent, might seem to the partner like a fish bowl. The sense of the nonsense of the politics of the porch!

The Eyes of Others

The witnessing presence of others co-constitutes concerns about the deed. Someone else might be physically present and watching you and your partner. Or an imaginary gallery of spectators might hover: frowning parents, moralizing priests, or howling friends. Adolescents anguish about their imagined appearance to referent others. Their eyes reduce the possible kiss to a performance.

The first other to deal with, of course, is the prospective kissing partner. Typically, the inexperienced adolescent believes that the potential partner is more practiced, worldly, and therefore bound to rate the kiss.

The peer group which "sanctions kissing" also cogenerates the pressure to do it. Faced with actual or imagined judgmental pressure, the adolescent is apt to decide to kiss as often to impress or to ward off ridicule as to act out of heartfelt desire.

In the Midst of the Wait

While plagued by such perplexing questions and petrified by ignorance of mechanics, youngsters grope for guidelines. They scrutinize kissing scenes on MTV. If they should stumble across a how-to-do-it kissing cookbook, they practically memorize it. They even try to rehearse what eludes rehearsal. "I used to practice kissing the bathroom mirror. It did nothing for my unexercised form. But straining to catch the moment of contact damn near made me cross-eyed." Some endeavors are more dramatic or drastic. Frequent stories told of "kissing cousins" or two same gendered chums practicing on each other are awkward and even sexually arousing. In contrast to remaining in a state of dazed languor, scanning for clues seems productive. But it resolves nothing. There is no cure for the wait.

In the Moment of the First Kiss

In a seeming paradox, descriptions of kiss happening do not always highlight the physical act itself. Some who report the kiss say they have no memory of the actual moment of lip contact. Obviously, this finding is a stumbling block to the research paradigm of mainstream behavioral science. How might the traditional psychologist observe, measure, manipulate, or make predictions with no behavioral data of the kiss? However, since I am not stuck with a bias in favor of measurable behavior, I have immediate access to the realization that this absence is a positive, revelatory phenomenon. How so?

In the midst of kissing, the kiss itself recedes into the background precisely because other themes stand out as figures. The sense of the kiss, its meaning and direction, embeds within the following three interrelated themes.

Self-in-situation

The beginner's awareness of self-in-the-act-of-performing might be the most thematic aspect in the immediate moment. Even as two sets of pilgrim lips are meandering toward a fateful collision, the adolescents are often dazed by unfamiliarity. The preoccupation with the self as performing shows in nervous giggles, tongue-tied awkwardness, "bad breath" concerns, or images of possible telltale lipstick stains.

Embodied Self

Embodied aspects also erupt with particular prominence. The body "blushes in heat" or "trembles in chill." It announces itself with parched lips, butterflies, lightheadedness, rubbery knees, dry mouth, dry throat, sweaty palms, heart palpitations, or a queasy stomach. Typical expressions include:

> There was so much to deal with in switching from side to side, in being careful not to smash noses, in trying to figure out what to do with excess saliva, with my tongue and with my hands. No wonder it gave me a headache. No wonder I gave her one too.

And another description:

> I was trembling so badly my teeth were chattering and my whole body was shaking like a leaf. It got worse when I noticed that she was trembling too. "I'm cold,"

I said, finally. She replied, tripping on the words, "How can you be, it's plus 88 degrees F scale?"

Context as Figural

Figure and ground reverse. The halo that surrounds the first kiss is often so vivid that it eclipses the actual moment of lip contact and obliterates any retrospective awareness of it. The kiss itself is a "blur." But incidents and feelings that surround it are vivid: the effort "to figure out the geometry of it" or the sense of "being caught guard and disoriented." One comical description illustrates vividly the typical way in which aspects of the situation can upstage the kiss itself:

> He reached to bring me closer to him and I noticed some scum on the corner of his mouth and thought "Yuk!" Then our lips began to meet. All I can remember is that the kiss was "French." After our lips parted I found myself carrying his scum on the corner of my mouth! I still thought, "Yuk!" That kind of bothered me. Actually it grossed me out! That's so ironic 'cuz here we were exchanging saliva which didn't bother me, yet I couldn't hack the other stuff from his mouth.

The vividness of the context might emerge as "mysteriously transcendent," too.

> I remember standing near to him. It was as though the physical space between us was alive and we each bordered that space and looked into it. Usually we had only chitchatted about inane things. Then we stopped talking for what seemed a long time. The silence was as active as speech.

Sometimes the context becomes salient precisely because one or both of the kissing pair become aware of the visible of the invisible or of the invisible of the visible.

The Moment of Disengagement

In whatever way the kiss occurs, there comes a pause, too brief or imperceptible to measure, but definite. Within that interval, the initial touch must be transformed. Either the dance of lips continues or the kiss ends. And no matter how the adolescents negotiate that pause they come eventually to the border of leave-taking. The first kiss inevitably ends.

How does one stop after a terrific first kiss? How does one retrieve a bungled attempt? What do you say to someone who has just bestowed on you the original kiss of your life? How do you look your partner in the eye afterwards? How do you "break from" a kiss that is overwhelming you?

F. Scott Fitzgerald describes the uncanny aftermath of Amory's first kiss: Curiosity yields to revulsion, disgust, and loathing for the incident; the urge to creep out of his body and to hide away follows the moment of quivering desire. Anger, stubbornness, and bruised vanity flair. Wonderful images fade. Instead of the sense of munching new fruit or watching the brush of young wild flowers in the wind, Amory stands stunned, staring helplessly at Myra "as though she were a new animal of whose presence on the earth he had not heretofore been aware" (Fitzgerald, 1920/1970,14-15).

The Aftermath

Accounts of the after-effects of the kiss range from wonderful to dull to revolting. What makes the difference? The experience of the outcome hinges not on the act of the kiss itself but on its meaning for the subject. There is a subtle two-way street between the existential stance of the adolescent before the kiss, the total context within which it transpires, and the outcome.

Some adolescents anticipate their first kiss, haunted by the presence of its absence. Others are not concerned about the issue at all. Why not? The attitude of expectation is interlaced with certain life-contexts. The cardinal variable is the ambiguous relationship between objective and lived time. Calendar age and readiness mesh to co-create anticipation. Suddenly, one youngster feels "colossally curious." Another has just discovered flirting. Still another begins "to see the world through romantic lenses." A female stops feeling like a tomboy, starts agonizing about her appearance to males, becomes picky about clothing and precise about make-up. The male, who used to laugh mockingly with his pals about "smooching," suddenly starts to look at girls with different eyes and through a "fog of fantasies." He even joins the group in popping the question: "are you psychologically inclined to be osculated?" He even buys deodorant for the first time.

Anticipated Kisses

The sanctioned-structured kiss: Party games
Peekaboo, hide and seek, and tag show the importance of games within our psychological economy. One ready-at-hand way of making relative the monumental issues about kissing is to concoct a game of it.

The party game is a common context for first kisses. It initiates the adolescent into this new behavior in a structured way. By definition, games disclaim the seriousness of any interflow between or among participants. Although a game does not totally resolve all ambiguities or handle perfectly all questions, it eases them. The levity of the game, of course, its practiced nonchalance is only a thin sunshade for its deadly earnestness. Still, it guarantees minimal incrimination and guards against any undesired self-disclosure. In agreeing to play, one merely follows the mood of the group. The tacit contract allows kissing by rules but permits nothing else. One is not voicing a personal choice, making any commitment, or expressing any desire to engage in extra-game or extra-party kissing. One only does like everyone else in the way everyone else does it.

The party kiss, therefore, is apt to be safe. It is exchanged either in front of all or in a designated spot, where privacy is flimsy and short lived. If any kiss last too long, a chorus of "razzing catcalls" from the next room or the other side of the drapes reminds the kissing partners of the nearby miniature multitude. Noise and laughter are props that surround all participants. The kissing game provides clear boundaries. Nothing need get too far out of hand.

> We played "spin the bottle." The kisses were not pecks!
> The winners of the spin, often rigged, would go off
> into the next room and emerge flushed and breathless
> minutes later. There was such a sense of walking on
> mysteriously dangerous ice, but there was such safety
> in numbers.

In spite of the structure, even the party kiss is not risk-free. In the act of participating, one might get more than one bargains for.

The natural kiss

Some adolescents are ripe and ready to kiss. If their personal intentions are fulfilled within a flowing context and harmonious relationship, the first kiss feels natural. Everything about the total situation fits. Even if the kiss happens by surprise, it seems pleasantly inevitable or "destined."

The aftermath of the natural first kiss is an afterglow: elation, jubilation, and a feeling of pride. "It felt so smooth. I walked home on cloud nine immensely pleased with myself. Finally, I had something to boast about. Mission accomplished." Another male danced all the way home: "I was beside myself. Casanova was no match for me." And from a female perspective:

> The moment was perfect. It felt blissful to be kissed for
> the first time ever and kissed French to boot! O-o-o

la-la. I felt on the top of the world and could hardly wait to describe it to my girlfriends. Now I knew the unknown and could speak with the voice of authority.

Another female writes: "The experience was so gentle that I was in awe. I walked back to my cabin on weak knees. My girlfriends told me I was blushing furiously. I felt lightheaded but oh so satisfied."

The disappointing kiss

For some who anticipate it, the kiss does not match their fantasies about the right person, the appropriate situation, or the act itself. One female acknowledges that she was looking for a "knight in shining armor." The guy in question, however, didn't fit the bill. He did not impress her. But while they were dancing, someone turned off the lights and she stumbled in the dark.

> He kept me from falling, and then his lips groped for mine. That was my first kiss. I can remember feeling like I was standing outside myself. Inside I screamed: 'He kisses like a fish! I gotta get out of here. All my fanciful dreams were shattered at age fifteen.

A disenchanting letdown is often inescapable. In light of the nerve racking build-up, a precise fit between expectation and event is difficult to realize. "I thought to myself that maybe it's not all it's cracked up to be," a female muses. "The words of an old song kept running through my head: 'Is that all there is'? I went home more puzzled than ever."

The contrived kiss

Adolescent curiosity often precedes desire. Over eagerness prods some youngsters to "force" the initial kiss. One male describes his "elaborate game plan executed without emotion. I never would have forgiven myself if I had let the opportunity pass. So I kissed her. But my heart wasn't in it. The experience felt pushed."

Artificiality marks kisses devoid of sensuality, ones motivated by "adventure seeking," "intrigue," or the "thrill of conquest." The novelist writes:

> . . . it was ordinary . . . he had expected more glamour. He had read many descriptions of love, and he felt in himself none of that uprush of emotion which novelists described; he was not carried off his feet in wave upon wave of passion; nor was Miss Wilkinson the ideal: he had often pictured the great violet eyes and the alabaster skin of some lovely girl, and he had thought of himself burying his face in the rippling masses of her auburn hair. He could not imagine himself burying his face in Miss Wilkinson's hair; it always struck him as a little sticky (Fitzgerald, 1920/1970, 142).

A male remembers feeling "led around by a perpetual erection" during early adolescence. He orchestrated his first kiss certain he had the mechanics down pat. But under the contrived circumstances, his curiosity wanes. Lust never erupted. "I couldn't believe how lust-less it was. It was one time in a row for being around a girl without an erection. She might as well have been my sister. I learned that you can't quarterback a kiss."

At twelve years old at summer camp, she was curious and romantic but not yet passionate. But she "set up" the most popular male camper. Listen to her series of maneuvers: "One rainy day I was lying on the couch in the Recreation Hall reading a comic book poised in such a way that he was bound to notice me." Later she manipulated him into an ambiguous conversation, "stilted but strangely different from our previous talks."

Later, he escorted her to her cabin after the marshmallow roast. She "stepped up one step to subtly accommodate for the height differences." He kissed her; she "performed." "I mentally stepped back, thinking: 'no rockets, fireworks, music or stars'. I faked enjoyment to humor him. But I felt nothing. Later, I sat on my bed contemplating becoming a nun."

The staged kiss

Sometimes peers orchestrate the circumstances. Not a few parties or double dates are arranged for the specific purpose of helping to season an unpracticed friend. One male recalls the kiss "engineered" by his pals. He tried to feign nonchalance and pretend sophistication. The result was a disaster. He writes: "My first official adolescent kiss ranked up there with eating corn. It was awkward, sloppy and very uncomfortable." His judgment is severe: "I was a flop! I failed my friends, mankind, and the female race."

Another "raw" lad describes his predicament:

> My buddies set me up with a "blind date." She was supposed to be "fast, loose, and hot." I learned that night that some blind dates are blinder than others. The guys tried to coach me before I went on stage, asking if I was sure I knew what a "French kiss" is. "Shit, I should I'm Italian. It can't be that different." Well surprise! I did not know what in God's name to do with that thing that kept penetrating my teeth. I thought she was getting ill.

In the wake of the "mechanical and unrewarding" kiss he decided that he was unworthy of his "Latin blood."

Unexpected kisses

Reaching the teen years does not automatically grant kissing a place within one's scheme of things. Some chronological adolescents still are psychologically juvenile as I described in Chapter Four. These youngsters experience their first kiss even though the wish to kiss has not yet entered into their desires, dreams, or daydreams. The following are types of unanticipated kisses.

The naïve kiss

She thought that she was ready, but admits

> I "flunked" my first kiss! It had never occurred to me
> to analyze how to kiss. I had no intention of doing it.
> There I was with my lips pursed when he approached
> me with his mouth open. The result was that his lips
> 'kissed' the skin surrounding my lips. Needless to say,
> my pursed lips were stuck in the middle. This went on
> for what felt like an eternity. He must have been lost
> in what he was doing and did not realize for several
> seconds that we were not lip to lip. I was dreadfully
> embarrassed at obviously being a novice.

The spontaneous kiss

This story starts from the perspective of innocent naïveté. Darlene
and Ron were eighth graders playing with peers in the winter's
first snowfall. Somehow, he and she became detached from the
rest of the group.

> In the midst of the struggle to rub snow in each others'
> faces, he put her down on a blanket of snow and then,
> as if riding a magic carpet, rolled half-beside her and
> half on top. Astonishingly, he began to lick the melting
> snow off her face. Darlene sensed the cold against her
> lower back where snow had slid under her coat and
> sweater. Intuitively, she knew the cold only indexed
> the heat they were generating. Her cheeks, caressed by
> his tongue, were burning.
>
> Ron licked, as if infinitely thirsty. His hands, feeling
> alive yet alien, moved upward and down. Deliriously,
> he searched her skin so easily accessible because of
> the cut of the clothing in fashion. Without thinking,
> he had shed his gloves and his darting fingers, like

icicles, torched her flesh. Darlene was becoming wet, wet where her clothes were most dry. She wanted to whisper, "Higher, Ron! Lower!" But they were kissing, and her voice was only forming soft sobs and whimpers. She began chewing on his tongue and moving her body so that his hands would keep moving, hoping they would touch her damp place. However, when his fingers did slip so low he touched hair, in shock he pulled away.

Their eyes, peering through a thin curtain of snow, posed searing questions: "*What* did we just summon between us? *How* did we do it?" The moment was detached from everyday time: They had exploded at each other from a place where they didn't even know they had been living. Both knew it, without thinking. They had to leap over the chasm their contact had already jumped—if they were to get back to being just kids . . . at play. It was so unexpected. It was too soon . . . . Both were dimly aware that their *hour* had not come . . . . Come Monday, they would begin to *not* talk about it again . . . ever . . . . Like each snowflake, it was one-in-a-row (Alapack, 2010b, 96-97).

The stolen kiss

His first kiss stunned an unripe male. He has a summer job as a counselor at a scout camp. One of the young cubs asked to take a picture of him with a particular female counselor.

As the boy camper was getting ready to shoot his picture I felt a something against the corner of my mouth. I turned my head to look and got the kiss smack on the lips as the camera flash went off. I was so shocked, embarrassed, confused and tongue-tied that I didn't even kiss back.

Alienating Kisses

I was the proverbial "sweet sixteen" lass. Stupidly I said, "I don't know how to kiss." He said he was gonna teach me. I was tense. It was a 'peck' at first. I had no idea of what to do with my hands. I felt humiliated that I had to be told where to put them. Then, it turned into a 'guided tour.' I couldn't wait till this 'memorable experience' was over.

I was shaking and blushing from head to foot and feeling helpless. At first, I was alarmed when his tongue started exploring my mouth. I didn't expect the moving of his hands all over my body, or the moving of his hands to move my hands all over him. He started breathing heavier. I felt a heat come over me. It made me feel profoundly ashamed. I wanted to slap his face.

The assaultive kiss

Some unexpected kisses can physically and psychically bruise. One young woman had a summer job at a Biblical Wax Museum. A much older man frequented it and would stop to chat with her. One evening, he stayed until closing time to help her lock up. She was wary as she finished her chores. As they walked out of the building, she sought a quick getaway. The stranger moved toward her, held her, forced his tongue into her mouth, and started to paw her.

Somehow, I managed to tear myself away from him. Stupidly, I said 'goodbye' and walked away quickly, yet, trying to give the impression of a nonchalant stroll. As soon as I hit the end of the block, I turned and ran as fast as I could with tears streaming down my cheeks. But I had to stop. Fortunately, I spotted a trash can nearby. Fortunately, I reached it in time before I started to vomit. The shock of the assault paled in significance to my lingering feelings: a shadow of hurt, a glimpse of fear, the invasion or rape, and the sense that my dandelion possibilities had been penetrated by a longing tongue.

The revolting kiss

A first kiss can be so incongruent that it revolts. She was fourteen years old, "in the last careless, carefree summer of my girlhood . . . He kissed me violently and pawed me all over. When I started to cry, he let me go." She has captured the sense of all premature first kisses:

> I didn't want it to count. I wanted to wipe it off as I rubbed off the saliva. I couldn't. It couldn't be reversed; I couldn't be un-kissed again. And the moisture, I could feel it, smell it, even though it was wiped. It made me nauseous. I started to gag. Then, as if at a primitive level my body was rejecting the assault, I threw up.

Retrospective Reflections

The immediate outcome of the first kiss does not exhaust its meaning. Across the distant clearing of time, it gains long term significance. Thoughts from a retrospective perspective either locate the individual within the event itself, or else situate the kiss within the totality of one's adolescence. Reflection uncovers three general categories:

A Big Step

The first kiss signifies "a milestone," "a major lesson in life," "a discovery of a new aspects of self," "a step on the road to womanhood." Negotiating this "step" or "hurdle" yields the sense of growing up, of cutting apron strings, of feeling older, more mature, and more seasoned.

A Rite of Passage

Our de-ritualized society celebrates no clear or distinct puberty rites. As "a momentous transition," the first kiss constitutes a "micro-rite or mini-ritual" (Alapack, 1975, 198) marking the way to a place within the unexplored world of adult feelings and relationships. "If this is what kissing and closeness are, then maybe the adults' world of sexual intimacy isn't so frightening."

The Harbinger of Adult Sensuality-Sexuality

While tracking the kiss from the strain of the rehearsal to the pain of the main event in the so-called battle of the sexes, I found libidinal issues conspicuously absent in this debut into grownup intersexuality. Exploration and discovery rather than passion or sensual pleasure comprises the glory for which the adolescent is bound by embarking upon the journey to the kiss. In the midst of the giggles, blushes, slurps, and sighs that sprinkle the first kiss situation, Eros is not thematic. One merely "flirts with an un-kindled fire." The kiss is a forerunner or harbinger that adumbrates sensual-sexual possibilities. The inaugural kiss "touches the tip of the iceberg. Whatever is next?"

General Structural Meanings

The structure of the first kiss shows two faces. Reflection upon the kaleidoscope of questions, images, feelings, meanings, and outcomes, reveals two general types of subjectively lived coherent patterning.

The Finite Kiss

The finitude of the kiss refers to its self-centeredness. An over-arching attitude of coiled concern with one's own expectations and needs obliterates awareness of, care for, and sharing with the other person qua unique other. The finite kiss dichotomizes the pair into split poles: subject and object instead of equal partners.

Self-pole

Self-esteem and social prestige form the twin motive for seeking the finite kiss (Alapack, 1984, 116). The aim is goal-directed. I kiss in "plain selfness" (Rubin, 1967/1977, 43). I kiss "to experiment," "to seduce successfully," "to boast about the conquest," "to become the envy of peers," or to prove that I am "not one of the ugly ones." A lust motivated kiss is finite, too, whether I initiate it, or am the recipient of another's lustful actions.

Other-pole

The finite pattern blurs the other's radiant face. I kiss a representative other not a particular Thou. The other is just "someone," "anyone whomever," "a convenient, willing, or available partner," merely an "accidental" occasion to kiss. A common statement of chance expresses this pattern of finitude: "I got lucky." Rubin (1977/1967, 43) describes this attitude graphically as a "self contentment containment absorption."

The Infinite Kiss

Within the infinite orientation, the accent falls on the mystery of the differences between the genders. The infinite kiss is transcendent and incipiently "other-centered and relationship constellated (Alapack, 1984, 115). Readiness to kiss and ripeness between self and other meld in the existential moment. The infinite kiss hyphenates the kissing pair into I-Thou.

The interflow

A careful and caring kiss from the heart allows me to escape my own sphere and overcome my "allergies" to the other-gendered person. Literally, I "face and taste" the magnificent, mysterious other and, wonderful to relate, my Thou reciprocates by facing and tasting back. Such a kiss is a simple, concrete, direct, and truthful taste of trust. It is an authentic advent that unlocks the existential doors to the possibility of physical closeness. I am "awe-struck by the power of just one kiss." Mundane saliva is transformed into "holy water that graces my lips" (Alapack, 1986).

F. Scott Fitzgerald (1925/1953, 112) characterizes both this transcendent movement of being captivated by the mystery of the kissing event and setting, and the sense of being absorbed in the awe of the other:

> His heart beat faster and faster as Daisy's white face came up to his own. He knew that when he kissed this girl and forever wed his unutterable visions to her perishable breath, his mind would never romp again like the mind of God. So he waited, listening for a moment longer to the tuning-fork that had been struck upon a star. Then, he kissed her. At his lips' touch, she had blossomed for him like a flower and the incarnation was complete.

Within this infinite attitude, I am able to "suck in the pap of life, gulp down the incomparable milk of wonder" (Fitzgerald, 1925/1953, 112).

The Kiss as Epiphany

> She bent over him, putting out a hand to his shoulder, and their lips met. Under her palm, she felt a tremor in his big frame. What she had first observed that Carney was, in a single word, innocent, came to her now with force. And she kissed him again with an almost maternal solicitude, as if it were he and not she who needed protection from the world. He did not attempt to rise and take her in his arms, as another man might have done. He did not move, lying on the grass, supported on an elbow, with his face upturned, accepting the touch of her lips and fingers in a kind of wonder, as if they had both fallen under a happy spell

that one word or gesture on his part would shatter (Raddal, 1963/1982, 74).

In Shakespeare's (1595/1980, 1073) classic romance, he puts words of eager gentleness in Romeo's mouth as he speaks to Juliet: "My lips, two blushing pilgrims, ready stand to smooth that rough touch with a tender kiss." An infinite kiss can also introduce one to an original experience of loss:

> Was it because she took my first kiss, that she took away my life's breath? Was it that she lied and [deceived] that one day suddenly the scales fell from my eyes and I saw a Medusa's head, and I saw life as a thing of terror? (Stang, 1979, 107).

If we rip out of context descriptions of "perfect" kisses, "magic moments," and "celebration," they sound sentimental, naïvely idealistic, or romantically tragic. But the heart of the matter is the couple's *basic enterprise* rather than the explicit kiss or its specific atmosphere. Rubin (1967/1971, 122) links the infinite kiss with mutuality when he describes "kissing . . . as if everything in each of us went out and in to both of us."

CHAPTER TEN

Kissing in General

Quintessential Intimacy

The kiss is an expressive act of touch. It is often sexual but not always. When it takes place within a sexual context, no sexual act is more intimate than kissing. Sexual intercourse involves touch, expresses one's self, and can be intimate. But the kiss is more personally expressive than intercourse. A kiss can mean more than a climax.

How can I justify such assertions? First and foremost, a kiss must be reciprocated. A kiss that is not bi-lateral is a failure. It is an aborted attempt. A true kiss is only when my partner kisses me back and a dance takes place of lips and maybe tongues. Loan-words from the French language carry this point. The French tongue differentiates between two types of pleasure, *plaisier* and *jouissance*. Whenever two pairs of lips meet, sensitive mucous membranes trade pleasure, but that does not exhaust the significance of the event. A mutual kiss also grants *jouissance*, which is genuine and uplifting satisfaction; pleasure plus (Lacan, 1966/1977). We can never reduce the significance of any sexual action to tension-reduction or homeostasis. A deep relationship with one's partner makes all sexual acts more personally satisfying. Some descriptions put flesh on these bones:

> I think kissing is the most intimate act between a man and a woman. You can only truly kiss someone when you really love them. When I kissed the first time, it

was really exciting and it is still exciting now. I wanted to go on forever because it felt so good.

"I had always wanted to kiss her, so when I kissed her for the first time; it was like an answer to a prayer. And it feels like a fire is building up in me slowly. Her lips are never enough for me. Sometimes I feel like swallowing her and I even forget to breathe sometimes."

> I can feel the depth of love we have for each other from a kiss. When I kissed the first time I was nervous but after the ice was broken I wanted more. I believe kissing is the best indicator of how much you love a person. It is really an intimate thing. And when you kiss someone, it carries along with it a taste, smell, or feeling that always reminds you of the person.

The Taste of Truth

Does not the way we kiss each partner existentially diagnose our relationships? A common complaint of couples in marital therapy, or at a marriage enrichment seminar or workshop, is "We don't kiss anymore." A quick peck on the fly replaces the oral indulgence that they used to savor. And a common realization of a couple that chooses divorce is that the end of the marriage showed in the kiss.

The kiss cannot be faked. Either we are 'in' the kiss or it is empty and cold. There is no place to hide while kissing, and no way to camouflage heartfelt emotions. Whenever someone detaches, withdraws, or tries to pretend a feeling, the partner senses it immediately and unerringly. "Kiss me as if you mean it," the discerning partner responds to a lack of enthusiasm or downright coldness. "Why did you turn your head?" "You stiffened when I held you." "Please don't close your mouth." "You kissed me like you were kissing your sister." "What's wrong? Did the cat steal your tongue?" A kiss not shared is nothing . . . or worse than nothing.

It is also easier to feign emotional responses during sexual intercourse. The latter can be sheer coupling performed without passion or tenderness and without union of hearts, bodies, minds, and souls. We all look beautiful or handsome in the dark. Just kill the light. We can experience powerful pleasurable sensations with anyone . . . with a total stranger, with someone who is drunk, even during a 'quickie' in the toilet at the disco on a Friday night in New York City. Rape is the worst-best example. You can force a kiss, but not the other's response.

Look at it from another angle. Western men during locker room talk use more than a few pathetic macho phrases while yapping about women. One such expression goes, "It doesn't matter is she isn't a 'perfect 10' or even a measly 'four'. Just put a paper bag over her head." That demeaning phrase makes the point perfectly. If a man did cover a woman with a paper bag, obviously he could not kiss her. He does not, of course, actually use the bag. The attitude, however, betrays pathetic disrespect. It reveals an aim is of getting a good "lay" or "a piece of ass." "Screwing." we call it, or "banging," "balling," or "jumping bones." The image of the paper bag, therefore, denigrates a woman.

A woman also can indulge in sexual intercourse without intimacy. I'm not just referring to prostitution. I mean that any woman can easily fake orgasm. By going through the motions of pretending to climax, a woman equally does violence to the man—even if her intention is to please him, inflate his virility, or flatter his ego.

Herein, I pen no commercial for sex only within marriage, and show no typical western dread of raw passion. Non-intimate sexual acts pepper daily life and season it well. Performance for performance sake requires no justification. Lust is a jewel that needs no apology. Anyone for some finite reason might choose a de-valued sex partner and prefer performance over meaning. Who can honestly gainsay that choice without knowing the whole situation? My point is that a reflection upon kissing reveals a key conceptual distinction between sexuality as expression or meaning and as behavior or performance.

Like the blush, therefore, the kiss is truth-telling. The kiss detects existential truth, truth as we live it, the kind of truth that orients our lives and helps us to get a beat on what might be happening between me and a cherished other. Truth, however, can be a bitter pill to swallow. No wonder that doers and thinkers say that it is akin to death (Lacan, 1949/1977). The magic of touch, in a 'moment', can turn tragic. One kiss is all it takes. We will return to this idea when discussing the relationship between the hickey and the vampire.

The Seriousness of Starting

From the perspective of abstract thought, the kiss seems trivial. As soon as you "taste" it, however, the whole world of love opens up . . . or closes down. How so? The kiss is an initiating act. It starts a lot for us. As an originating act, the kiss surprises us. I invent a piece of qualitative algebra when I say. "In the beginning was the kiss" (Alapack, 2001). We might not be aware of romantic feelings for a person until we "surprisingly" kissed. After we break the moment and open our eyes we both knew. Our shared look shows that it will never again be the same between us. We just changed each other's lives. D.H Lawrence (1922/1969, 331) expresses it this way, "he kissed her on the mouth, gently, with the one kiss that is an eternal pledge . . . He had crossed over the gulf to her, and all that he had left behind had shriveled and become cold."

> She approached me, put her arms around me, and drew my lips to hers. It was exquisitely gentle. "This is long overdue," she said, and we kissed again. We munched. At least, I munched on her lips. It seemed like she munched on mine, too. Then we stopped as naturally as we had begun. "It was a feast," I said. "I've been to a banquet." "Sure as shooting," she said, sounding like a pixie . . . . [Then she kissed me again], this time more softly, so softly that any softer would have felt like a dream. "We'll always remember today," she said.

Richard J. Alapack

Looking at each other across a clearing wide enough
for seeing clearly, neither of us had to voice the living
question that hovered between us: "Where in the world
did the two kids just go?" (Alapack, 2007, 33-34).

Every time we kissed, I thought to myself "These lips
are strange, and they will be always. Why do they feel
so familiar?" Talk about kissing! That's how it started.
I met him at a social gathering at my church. Go ahead
laugh, if you think it's funny. But things like this do
happen, you know. Anyway, he asked me to go outside
with him. I forget now the pretext. I already mentioned
experiencing a threat rushing at me pell-mell from
out of the blue. As soon as we got outside the door of
the hall, he touched my shoulder. To my own shock,
I spun to face him. The first kiss was shy. The second
was the sort that innocent me could never possibly
have imagined. After we opened our eyes and stared
at one another, it was all over for me. Everything was
different and always would be. From a kiss like that
there is no going back. If you've never experienced it,
I don't know how else to communicate it. It was lethal.
It transformed my life (Alapack, 2007, 93).

Yukio Mishima (1973, 85) depicts the experiential
ache, like an amputation, that follows the end of a kiss
which in some significant sense is an originating or
transformative act:

It was like awakening reluctantly from sleep, struggling
drowsily against the glare of the morning sun as it struck
their eyelids, as they yearned to hold on to the fragment
of unconsciousness left to them . . . When their lips
parted, an ominous silence seemed to fall, as though the
birds had suddenly stopped their attractive song.

"I Was Robbed": The Missed Chance

In the preceding chapter, I presented "stolen kisses." To say they were unwanted does not even come close to capturing the feelings that my participant-subjects describe. Individuals also express their disappointment at unrealized kisses. The section titled "The Space of the Kiss" describes circumstances which turn a potential kissing situation into a botched beginning. Some individuals balk at the unrealized 'moment' and complain that they were "robbed":

> I was so ready to kiss him that I could taste it. But I never got to taste anything. I started to lean towards him, demurely, and even closed my eyes. Nothing happened. When I opened my eyes, he was gone. I'll never know what was going on, or not going on. But I felt embarrassed and gypped.

> I wanted to kiss her. She knew it. By the looks in her eyes, I could see her mind juggling "yes" and "no." When she dropped her eyes and took a step back, I knew "no" won. In my disappointment, I moved towards her and accidently touched her hand. I took that feeling home. But I felt cheated. I hate the word "no."

Memory is amazing. It surely cannot be reduced to a physiological trace. We never forget what did not happen. The truth of that statement is beyond biological explanation.

The Seriousness of Ending

Kisses also end 'things'. The missing passion or absent tenderness of a relationship has gone "dead" shows in the kiss. I can mouth all the 'right' words, tell you that I love you . . . and even believe I mean it. The truth, however, appears not in the verbal lines but in the cold and empty kiss. The way we kiss each partner existentially diagnoses our relationship. The kiss is a "lie detector" (Weitman, 1999, 76). The divorce lawyers enter whenever the question "Does the cat have your tongue" translates into "Who are kissing instead of me?"

Desire Consciously Expressed and Acted Upon

It suits to link kissing to phenomena we have considered thus far. Touch, we have seen, is indispensable in different ways and at different levels while playing peekaboo, or hide and seek, or tag. The kiss takes the extensiveness and intensity of touch one step farther. Lip-touch is more romantic and more erotic. As part the lust dynamism, kissing romanticizes our total body in both the anatomical-physiological and lived senses. After we tasted another's lips, no surprise, we all wanted more, didn't we? "More please," we asked, or at least thought to ourselves. And we didn't even know what 'more' we were aching for. But we found out, didn't we?

To hearken back to the revelations of the first kiss, remember that initially we didn't know how to do it 'right'. We didn't even know how to do it 'wrong'. Only after it happened and with some experience under our belts could we even see the complex spectrum of the kiss and appreciate the grey-zones of the good, the bad, and the ugly. We knew that "more" was a qualitative not a quantitative desire.

One of the loudest chants of this book is that in the affairs of human love and human sexuality we are never determined or helped by instinct. Biological data contributes some information to explaining human sexuality, but it does not adequately understand or comprehend it as a whole. In matters of managing or coping with the subtle but pervasive link between heart, head, and genitals, we make choices repeatedly. We take risks. Do we kiss or turn away? Do we engage in sexual intercourse, yes or no? Evolutionary psychology takes us on a dead end by lifting us into a flimsy cloud of pure abstraction. It simply cannot account for how we make such decisions. A beaver builds damns by instinct. The swallows come back to Capistrano by instinct. Mamma cat rolls over for Tomcat, never hesitating because of the possibility of pregnancy. Trying to balance heart, head, and genitals requires that we earthlings making choices. Each choice is a leap. Every leap has no guarantees. That is why in matters of the heart it is heaven or hell, agony or ecstasy. Natural science comprehends none of it.

The Kiss as Joining Together

The kiss is a true symbol that is what it signifies: a joining, mingling, or a fusion. Two become one flesh. We say, "You take my breath away." "I can't get enough of you." "I want to eat you up." "Such kisses that they must kiss each other for ever" (Lawrence, 1928/1983, 143).

> He walked near to her, and with the same, silent, intent approach put his arm round her waist, and softly, very softly, drew her to him, till his arm was hard and pressed in upon her; she seemed to be carried along, floating, her feet scarcely touching the ground, borne upon the firm, moving surface of his body, upon whose side she seemed to lie, in a delicious swoon of motion. And whilst she swooned, his face bent nearer to her, her head was leaned on his shoulder; she felt his warm breath on her face. Then softly, oh softly, so softly that she seemed to faint away, his lips touched her cheek, and she drifted through strands of heat and darkness. Still she waited, in her swoon and her drifting, waited, like the Sleeping Beauty in the story. She waited, and again footsteps lingered and ceased, they stood still under the trees, whilst his lips waited on her face, waited like a butterfly that does not move on a flower. She pressed her breast a little nearer to him, he moved, put both his arms round her, and drew her close. And then in the darkness, he bent to her mouth; softly, and touched her mouth with his mouth. She was afraid; she lay still on his arm, feeling his lips on her lips. She kept still, helpless. Then his mouth drew near, pressing

open her mouth, a hot, drenching surge rose within her, she opened her lips to him, in pained, poignant eddies she drew him nearer, she let him come farther, his lips came and surging, surging, soft, oh soft, yet oh, like the powerful surge of water, irresistible, till with a little blind cry, she broke away (Lawrence, 1915/1975, 297-298).

CHAPTER ELEVEN

The Hickey: The Embarrassing Badge of Burgeoning Sexuality[4]

What's the Hickey?

A hickey is a blatant mark on some part of the human body made by one person putting her or his mouth on another person's skin and sucking for a protracted period of time and with enough force to break the blood vessel beneath the skin, or the doer of the deed bites vulnerable flesh,

Although it depends upon the tone, shade, texture, and elasticity of one's skin, the hickey typically manifests a particular face or physiognomy. Initially, it displays mixed colors: "an awesome orb of raw—pink, purple, blue, and red flesh no bigger than a dime." Later on, it turns muddy yellow and maroon. It darkens and dulls as it gradually fades. At first appearance on the skin, a fresh hickey furnishes prominent and undeniable proof that two people—gay, lesbian, or heterosexual—had shared a fleshy encounter.

The hickey is literally and metaphorically a crude concrete 'bite', an 'intensive point' that marks "excesses" of pleasure, pride, pain, and torture (Lingis, 1983). In the "moment" one receives it, begins to "hold" it, touch it, and check it out it in the mirror, it feels raw, sore, and new—especially if it the first

---

[4] Technology and the body: Vanishing hickeys and the waning of adolescence. Presented to the *Sixteenth International Human Science Research Conference*, Trondheim, Norway, August 1997.

time ever wearing one. Sometimes the passion mark is invisible to the others. It is etched on the breast, chest, thigh, or near the genitals. One young woman calls her hickey "A sweet secret that excluded everyone else and sealed a pact between him and me." A young man writes that he and his lady "traded hickeys as tokens of commitment in the afterglow of our first intercourse." A fellow who earned his mark during the heat of passion titles his hickey "My Purple Heart."

The hickey is most often inscribed in a place where it flashes for the whole world to see. The "marked woman" hides her mark on her neck from her parents by donning a scarf or turtleneck sweater. By wearing an open-necked blouse, in another context, she flaunts the mark above her cleavage to selective friends or classmates. The hickey is a flashlight that one either wants 'on' or 'off', depending upon who is present to notice its glow.

To discover the range of meanings of the bite, I asked subjects, "Please describe an unforgettable episode when you either received or bestowed a hickey." I analyzed the written protocols using Amedeo Giorgi's (2007) descriptive phenomenological method.

Contexts of Bestowing or Receiving a Hickey

Curiosity

> At the time on our Island, Bermuda, my peers were suffering from "hickey fever." Curiosity kills the cat. Mine just got the better of me. I wanted something to "show off" just like my friends. So I asked Billy, the too eager boy-next-door, to give me one. He placed his wet slobbery mouth on my clean white skin and began to suck. I thought someone had turned loose on my neck a crazed vacuum cleaner with teeth! But the final results were absolutely marvelous! I have tender skin. So this mixture of purple, black, and red did a lot for my image. Now I, too, was "cool." Until it faded I wore my hickey as an accessory to my wardrobe.

Playing with Passion

Whenever I was flirting, I used the hickey as my "alarm clock" to mark the danger point and signal the end of passion for that particular night. I always stopped whenever I got one until a guy I really liked called me a "cockteaser." That night I ended up on my back, spread-eagle, with a hickey on a spot that nobody ever saw. Fortunately, I didn't end up with a baby or AIDS.

Manipulative Play

With teasing and tickling a situation begins playfully. With a taunting challenge it quickly becomes 'deadly serious': "I de-double dare you." One ends up either feeling "used" or "using" the other. The élan of getting a hickey signified for one girl the "consummation" of her relationship with the boy. She remarks, "When the hickey finally disappeared my vision of our perfect love also faded. It was weird. But the next time we were together, we broke up. I guess I had gotten what I needed from him."

It was the first time I had ever felt sexual while with a guy. I still remember the glowing feelings of my warm skin, his hot breath, and lethal whispering. A twisted spring ran through my interior from my vagina to the tip of my rib cage. The combination of being held tightly and the painful pleasurable wet sensations on my neck set the internal spring in action. The next day, when I looked in the mirror, I could not ignore the dark red hickey. The next day when I saw him, he ignored me.

Infinite Discovery

One seventeen year old fellow intended to venture "boldly where no man has ever before gone." He envisioned no deeper discoveries. But on his first serious girlfriend's fifteenth birthday, she wanted to do something "daring." He relates:

She encouraged, nay pushed me. I went with the flow. Eventually somehow I managed to get my hand under her bra and started to feel her up. Then I chickened out. But she yanked my hand back to her boobs and helped me unbutton her blouse. Then she stood up, took off her bra, faced me, and said. "Do you like them?" My jaw dropped. Next thing you know there's a nipple in my mouth! "Give me a hickey," she said. "Bite me." Locker room talks had taught me this was supposed to be my victory to be savored, my conquest to be relished. But it was not like that. I was not in control. She, not me, was enjoying the pleasure. She wanted the hickey. My perception of male-female sexual relations changed quickly from locker room "trash-talk." Her aggression knocked me off balance. New sexual thoughts filled my mind. Sex isn't a "me" enjoying it. Rather it's me enjoying her enjoying me . . . or any way you want to phrase it. Some activities are made worthwhile by the other person's enjoyment. Sexual conquest was no longer an option in my playbook. I would sit in the locker room after football practice and shake my head listening to the guys' macho blabber. In an eye-blink, my viewpoint about guys and girls switched.

Looking at and Handling the Hickey

Focus on the hickey's colorfully striking perceptual impact and emotional effect is another rich possibility available for reflection. The splendor and the horror of seeing!

First Sighting

"You gotta see it to believe it!" Upon first sight the stunning material visibility of the mark and its striking colors grab the eyes of the naïve but now troubled youngster. The first "bit of worry" is finding a way to "handle" this fleshy spot that already has seized me. As soon as I see it on my body or on the other's, intuitively I know that it will last awhile—although I am without cues concerning its longevity. Its glare and density seize my gaze. I begin to handle it with both fingers and eyes, touching it ever so gingerly and gently. Making contact with it is both perceptual and emotional.

Seeing It on the Flesh

Under what circumstances did it appear to me? How did it come into view?

> My girlfriend asked if I wanted a hickey. I didn't know what it was but didn't want to appear ignorant so I said, "Sure." After she administered the first one on my lower neck, I watched as its shape expanded from a small bright red mark to a more generalized larger red arch with a hint of blue. This was remarkable!

> My boyfriend started "sucking face." I purposely sunk to a lower position. I wanted this hickey to be visible for my friends to see. I wanted to make sure it would be prominently located: on the neck above the collar-line and sweater-line. I remember dashing quickly to the bathroom to check it out. It looked marvelous, something to brag about!

Looking into the Mirror

Vision again! One might see it first in the mirror after it has already taken form . . .

When we were making out, I felt her warm mouth on my neck. I didn't know what she was doing. The next morning I awoke and went into the bathroom. In the mirror I saw a dark hickey at the base of my neck. I did a double take "Man," I said under my breath, "You're in big trouble." There was no way I was going to let her parents see it. They'd know exactly what we'd been doing.

I was young and innocent when I got my first hickey. Giving and receiving them that night was totally spontaneous. They happened unexpectedly the first time we made love. I don't even think that I even knew what they were before that. I saw it in the bathroom mirror the next morning. I called it a "love—tattoo" that marked our first intercourse. With the hickey she gave me a part of herself to carry around. That purple-ish, yellow-ish mark on my neck to me looked awesome.

In the Words or Gaze of the Third Party

Here comes the power of the look once more. Sometimes the hickey is not discovered until a third party spots it, comments on it, or asks about it. It is doubly awkward for the adolescent to see it only after it is first pointed out by another. The third party is usually a family member, friend or peer—commonly one's mother.

I didn't know he had put his mark on me. I had felt hot, heavy breathing and a damp sensation on my skin while we were necking. I just thought his breath was condensing or that the feeling was his lips on my neck. When I arrived home my younger but more experienced brother asked me about my new "bite." I was shocked and embarrassed especially since I was so clueless. It suddenly felt very "gross" and dirty.

The day after he planted one on my neck, I was wearing my pajamas at breakfast. Do I have to mention that they were not turtle-necked? I was unaware of what had happened. My mother noticed my ugly welt and asked me what had happened to my neck. I don't know where my quick response came from, but I said I got hit by a ball on the playground. She rolled her eyes, but let it go at that.

Mamma's Knowing Eyes . . .

however, do not always radiate such easy acceptance.

My first hickey coincided with my first sexual intercourse. Flashing like neon it announced to the entire world what I had done. My mother saw the awful spot as soon as she laid eyes on me. She knew, exactly. Disappointment and pain were written on her face. I felt guilty and ashamed. I had let us both down. I was only sixteen years old. I wanted to be innocent and pure. The hickey was a concrete sign that what I had done I couldn't undo.

Daddy's Transparent Teardrop

I had wanted a hickey so badly for so long that I would have "put out" for it. Regretfully I did. That's how insecure I was then and how badly I wanted to be desired by a boy. My hickey was a juicy gem shining like Rudolph's red nose right on my neck. I'll never forget my father's crushed look upon seeing it, followed by a tear rolling down his cheek! It was the first time I ever saw my father cry. T-o-r-e me up. Suddenly I was humiliated and ashamed. I was supposed to be "daddy's girl." Why was I feeling like a "scarlet woman" wearing my scars?

Grandparents' Looks of Concern

I was almost sixteen and wanted a hickey badly. All the "cool" guys had a few. To get me some I took out this girl with a reputation as "fast" and "easy." Actually it was the first time I felt bare tit and got inside a female's pants, too. I was in "Seventh Heaven." Well, the first one to see my "delectable marks" was my grandmother. I almost laughed when she blurted, "Oh, my God, oh no, Andrew, you can get cancer from hickeys!" But then she got pale and had to sit down. I got worried. What if she had a heart attack! In a flash I felt grossed out by the blue welts on my neck. Now it seemed like a personal insult that fruit of my acts should be on display on my neck. When me-maw's eyes met mine, I blushed, double proof of my guilt. I was ashamed. I felt like a doubly marked man.

Side Glances of the Peer Group:

I woke up early and rushed to look in the mirror to see how large it was. I was so excited. I went to school showing it off by wearing a low-cut blouse. On the bus I was on cloud nine and unable to stop grinning or looking in my compact mirror at the large and very noticeable marks on my neck. But by the end of the day I was trying to cover it up. I spent the whole day blushing because I was so embarrassed by the condemning looks and actions of my friends. I was sporting a hickey. But I was still a virgin. Their responses made me feel like a cheap slut. I wanted the marks to go away. I felt humiliated and stupid. Later in my bedroom I stared in the mirror again at those disgusting hickeys. They made me cringe. How I hated them! I tried to wipe them away. My gesture was futile.

CHAPTER TWELVE

Psychological Parables of the Hickey

Caught in a situational vortex

Consistent with my dealing with other phenomena, I offer elaborate narratives of the hickey. The parables will put more flesh on these bones and hot blood under these bruises. More importantly, they link the hickey to everyday life situations, ones that depict youngsters in trouble. In daily life the hickey indeed often triggers erotic trouble. Let me be clear. Adolescents do not necessarily go through their teen years battling or wallowing in Sigmund Freud's and G. Stanley Hall's period of "storm and stress." But being troubled by carnal eroticism does fit the young adolescent "moment." The marked body affects nearly every aspect of the young adolescent's existence. A rash of thoughts and emotions crowds one's life-space with confusion, distress, vexation, worry, and creates a cauldron of interpersonal dynamics.

The following parables also might help you decide for yourself what weight to give to this small mark, to this ugly bruise, to this gross welt, to this gorgeously delectable orb. Significant or trite: splendid or hideous.

Psychological Parable # 1: Branded

He got his first hickey at age fourteen years. His opening line announces his innocence: "In grade nine, the female gender was a mystery to me. My girlfriend, Brenda, was very knowledgeable. She showed me the ropes."

"One night she began kissing me. It wasn't on the mouth. My ears, neck, chest, and the side of my face were spots of prey. Wrapped up in the pleasure, I didn't realize what she was doing." These words confirm his innocence. They also show his complicity with his more experienced partner. Then, "with a look of condescending pleasure," she stops to check her handiwork. She shows what she had been fashioning. She does not just demonstrate her experience, but she also stakes a claim. "She said that now I was 'hers' because she had branded me. I went nuts! I couldn't believe what I saw. A scene flashed from an old Western movie of cowboys herding cattle to get burned by the iron."

Her smug possessiveness exasperates him, changing his mood and manner. He becomes highly emotional and with newfound defiance decides "Two can play this game." Less innocent now, he decides upon payback. But trying to give her a hickey humiliates him. She has to explain how to do it. "When I finally saw it on the side of her neck, it shamed me."

She smoothly short-circuits his bravado and thwarts his attempt to surmount his naïve complacency. She ropes him back to follow her lead into her self-styled round-up and into the pasture of her choice. Before this event, he had no concern about control. But now, silly and foolish, he knows that he lacks it. He is in a vortex; he is in trouble.

He's in double-trouble. "Wearing the hickey created another problem. I couldn't let my mom find out. She didn't really like Brenda in the first place. She would flip over what Brenda was doing with me." The vortex has sandwiched him between the two most important females in his life. Brenda ruffled his feathers, pushed his anger-button, and tightened her hold on him. Nevertheless, he doesn't want to lose her. At the same time, he's still very much attached to his mother. He's sure she will scorn the marks all over his body. They clearly prove her point that Brenda is not his "kind," but rather a dangerous girl he should not be involved with. And he figures that Brenda really flashed her look of smug satisfaction over her "artwork" more at his not-present mother than at him. Brenda won't be too pleased at his wish to hide the hickeys from his mom. This "raw material" and "material evidence" might lead either female "to cook my goose." He sees no exit to the swirl that has sucked him in.

While at home over the weekend, he succeeds in hiding his marks from his mother by wearing turtlenecks and high-collared shirts. But he isn't so sure that he successfully concealed from Brenda his need to hide them. Brenda asked several pointed questions about his clothing. To placate her—or to try to deceive her, just as he had had to deceive his mother—he goes to the other extreme around the kids he grew up. He tells Brenda, "Around my friends I flaunted your classic marks, proud to show them off." He feels better about this openness because he had never before had to handle a tangled rope of lies.

He paraded them alright. But both Brenda and he miscalculated. His bravado boomerangs. Responses from peers puncture his high-flying balloon of pride. The girls call him a "slime-ball," making it obvious that—like his mother—they figure he and Brenda are having sex. They give him the cold shoulder and shun him. The guys in the locker room just think it's funny. They tease him for being "pussywhupped" by Brenda, confirming his own images of "a steer being brought to the branding iron." They give him a "mock prescription." If he were a "real man," they say, he would seize the reigns from her and start "jumping her bones." They insinuate, however, that she is not going to let that happen. She is pulling his chain now and will "pull it that way" until she is ready. Brenda just laughs off his weak attempts to talk about the matters. Every which way he looks, there's trouble. He's tormented. What happened to the boy "with not a worry in the world?" With those hickeys she put my life into her wallet."

In the truest sense those hickeys never faded away. "We married. We had three kids. I never knew when she was apt to give another love-bite, or where. I learned to love the suspense and the playful intimacy."

Psychological Parable #2: The splattered grease alibi

We were in my room necking, acting goofy, teasing, and tickling each other. All of a sudden I noticed a large smirk on his face. He had been nibbling at my neck and then POW he did it. I was ready to kill him. Thoughts of wearing turtlenecks in the hot summer season immediately came to mind. A second ago innocence draped her. Now she slips into a vortex with trouble just beginning.

The next day proved interesting. He and I were at school in a room full of guys. Somebody said something about my turtleneck. The guys were giving my boyfriend winks and one even patted him on the shoulder like he had scored a game-winning goal at soccer! A look of pleasure came over his face; a look of pain covered mine. My face had never been so tomato-like before. The thought flashed, "They think I let him screw me!" It was like a heat-wave. I suddenly felt cheap. *Why didn't he blush?*

The gyre turns once more. Apparently she is still too indecisive to make changes. The next time it occurred, I was once again not ready. We were lying on my bed with him kissing my face. No problems, right? Wrong! He decided to give me a hickey on my eye. Wouldn't work? Wrong again. Why was he laughing? I got up to look in my mirror. My god, it was huge! This sucker bite of my selfishly cruel boyfriend had a lip-shaped form.

Following him back to school exposes her to more trouble. "There is no turtleneck made for eyes," she says, as if coining a cliché. Her friends assault her with intrusive questions. She concocts a story. "I was frying some onions and garlic to make hamburgers for lunch. The grease just splattered right into my eye socket." She insists, "That was the truth." She qualifies, "That was *my* truth." She sustains the lie. "Not even my best friends heard a different story until many years later."

The vortex draws her into deeper complications. What about her mother? She had easily covered the first hickey with turtleneck sweaters. Would her mother "buy the splattered grease alibi?" As soon as she saw her mom, and saw that her mom saw the mark below her eye, she stumbled on her "greasy lie" and broke into tears. Her mother jumped to the conclusion that she was crying because she had lost her virginity. "Mom started screaming that she was going to tell my father, that I was grounded, lost all my privileges, and that I was never going to see my boyfriend again." Listening to her mother rant and rave, she felt trapped in "somebody else's nightmare." The vortex slowed when her mother confessed that "she had gotten a hickey and lost her virginity at the same time when she was exactly my age simultaneously when she got pregnant with me." The spinning spiral finally stopped when they cried in each other's arms. Then she exited the twisting vortex by "terminating" the cruel, controlling involvement with her "first, serious boyfriend."

Reflections on the Hickey Encounter

What is behind the hickey? What motivates bestowing the bruise? Why do it? The language of the streets calls it a "love-bite," a "passion-mark," or a "fleshy tattoo." The common "buzz" about the mark polarizes in two opposite viewpoints. One view sees it as an instrumental act made for a strategic or even a manipulative purpose. An unabashedly possessive person makes a "sucker bite" in order to stake a claim. The raw red or dark purple hickey broadcasts the clear message to all: "He's mine"; "Hands off, bubba, she's with me"; "You can look, but don't even think about . . . touching her."

Jealous or controlling possessiveness, however, falls far short of exhausting the reasons for bestowing and receiving the mark. Another view imputes a romantic motive to the deed. The hickey is never only a mark on the skin. One receives the love-bruise with the fibers and the sinews of flesh. It is not made by the mouth and teeth alone but by the living heart. The hickey awakens and stirs the blood of my beloved. The act of giving it signifies that the captured is captured by the captured. Trading hickeys is a raw and vulnerable transaction eliciting pain that one can bear . . . again and again . . . . and again. I will return to this theme of the living blood in the next chapter when I link the hickey to the phenomenon of the vampire.

The preceding chapter told a long, elaborate, intensive, and extensive story of the broad spectrum of meanings and motives for the hickey. And the two parables about hickey encounters amplify the meaning of the badge. The hickey is basic sensual-sexual expressiveness, "the birth mark" of sexual awakening, *an unstable and embarrassing badge of burgeoning sexuality* (Alapack, 2001). A visible badge, yes, that one esteems as either splendid or hideous.

The obvious fact cannot be said enough: ***We cannot receive or bestow a hickey over the Internet.*** Much writing nowadays discusses the place of the body in cyberspace. Chapter seventeen deals with Online flirting and harkens back to these chapters on the hickey to differentiate Net interaction from raw encounters in the flesh. The hickey is pure skin and flesh, as far removed as possible from the text messages on Facebook, Twitters, or ordinary email. It differs completely also from indulgence in fantasy-images or "sex-in-the-head" communication. And it is equally removed from verbal "head games" such as phone sex or "phonication," voiced encounters, interactive videos, or chat room visits (King, 1996, 95).

The hickey differs, too, from the tattoo. It is transient. It glares, lasts for a protracted period of time, and then it naturally fades away. Patricia Mac Cormack (2006, 72) considers "the great ephemeral tattooed skin" a bodily vehicle to express counter-cultural attitudes of deviance or defiance. She calls the tattoo a "micro-political act." Because why? It is ephemeral by choice. It remains fixed until purposefully removed. But a hickey rarely makes a political statement. Two kids who trade them are not necessarily defying authority or trying to provoke grownups. The hickey is what it expresses and expresses what it is: mouth or teeth bruising skin. It has more to do with burgeoning sexuality than with making socio-political statements. If it defies, it defies viewpoints about sexuality, not about political corruption and corporate greed.

The hickey is precisely an ambiguously embarrassing emblem because, once one wears it on the body, one is temporarily stuck with it. Unlike the blush or the tattoo, it is materially resistant and lasts for a protracted period before it physically fades. Go to *Google* and you will find information that hickeys typically last from four to twelve days. During that interval, you cannot wish it away, blot it out, or rub it off. Thus, you are forced to deal with the implications and consequences of its presence. Indeed, its conspicuous *ultra-material sexuality* appropriates me. That is, it literally takes me over. Sooner or later, I must *appropriate this appropriation.* In some way or other, I must stamp this epiphany on my skin with my personal signature. It is mine. I have to own it.

To repeat, unlike the blush, which radiates and then quickly fades, the hickey persists. It is not like a fantasy image that swiftly drifts away with the wind or a text message that disappears at the click of a mouse. It does not vanish when one's computer system goes down. It lingers after the CD-ROM slides out of its slot. I can exit the chat room, turn off the tape, hang up the phone, or pull the plug but the hickey endures, tucked away under my scarf or turtleneck sweater. The make-up I apply won't successfully cover it. Sometimes it seems that it will last forever.

It suits to elaborate. Youngsters scrutinize and track the fluctuating mark. "I watched it turn from a red sore-look to a blackish yellowish bruise look and saw it shrink in size, blend into the color on my skin and gradually fade. At length, I witnessed its disappearance. I named it my "multiple fickle friend." Even after physically vanishing, like a painful phantom limb it stigmatizes the individual with reminders of pure glee . . . or broken promises.

The mark on the skin is a "double etch." What do I mean? It blots the skin. But it also indicates a transition. The first hickey steals innocence, just like the Biblical bite of the apple in Eden. A "young wolf has make his mark." *There* on the throat undeniably loiters a "fleshy tattoo." It glows like "a neon sign spelling S-E-X, thus broadcasting that momma's sweet young girl has been "had." A young maiden fashions "erotic handiwork with her "love-suck." She splatters "spots of prey" like glowing paint in shades of purple and crimson on the boy's neck or etched above the collar-line. Her hickey rests at the spot where the neck and the chin meet, or maybe right below the Adam's apple, or perhaps below the eye. The mark on body is vivid, equivocal, and emotionally laden.

It is hard to pinpoint a phenomenon better suited than the hickey to express the adolescent's ambiguous predicament of being troubled by lust dynamism. "Is it not the indecisive and equivocal carnality . . . . the indecisive carnal substance not yet held in resolved form that makes the awkward youth so troubling?" (Lingis (1985, 62-63). A young man and a young woman faced the implications of being bedecked with hickeys, become drawn into a painful whirlpool. Ron Cornelissen (Personal Correspondence) depicts such trouble precisely and eloquently. He says that "in the face of both external and internal 'conspiring events', adolescent lived space, lived time, and lived embodiment collapse into a "situational vortex." "One finds oneself in erotic trouble as in a dream," Lingis writes (1985, 65) "having forgotten why one came here or where one is going or what one had sought to obtain in passing this way."

CHAPTER THIRTEEN

A Comprehensive Understanding of the Hickey: Marks and Stains, Social-Cultural Rituals, and Historical Practices of Marking the Body

The meaning of a hickey is much broader that the mere trading of the "bite." A comprehensive exposition of the phenomenon must view it against the backdrop of at least three larger patterns or gestalts. The hickey belongs to: 1) marks and stains; 2) social-cultural rituals, rites, and traditions; 3) and various historical practices of flesh-branding during spectacles of public punishment.

What do I mean by marks and stains? They are ordinary trite cuts and spots, blots and blemishes, smears and scars. These commonplace phenomena are thoroughly concrete but also mean something that transcends them. A list, inclusive but not exhaustive, includes: the blush, blotches, and blemishes, beauty marks, freckles, pimples, and scars; pierced ears, ornamented body parts, tattoos, dyed-hair, body-paint; spotting at the menarche, ejaculation spots on pajamas, pen-knife incisions on "blood-brothers," the stain on the sheet after intercourse, stretch marks from childbearing; lipstick stains, ink spots, powder smudges; lust-lines, laugh-lines, wrinkles, crow's feet; the notches on the bedpost, the notches on the gun; autographs, doodles, graffiti, fingerprints . . . slashed wrists (Alapack, 1986).

The hickey also relates to an intensive and extensive cluster of non-western social-cultural rituals and traditions: acts of mutilation, tattooing, circumcision, body painting, cicatrization, clitoridectomy, scarification, perforation, and inscription (van Gennep, 1908/1975, 65-115).

Thirdly, the hickey is akin to historical practices of branding the flesh within ceremonial rituals of control, torture, exhibitions, and excesses (Lingis, 1983). It is associated to "the liturgy of punishment" by branding during public spectacle (Foucault, 1975/1979, 33ff). Add to these ties to folklore about vampires, stigmata on mystics, and to the permanent "crack in the wall" in the soul-scape of holocaust victims, hideous and heinous identification numbers burned into Jewish flesh by Nazi executioners (Kruger, 1966/1986). The neglected hickey belongs to a large family.

The hickey links most concretely and relevantly to passage rites (*rites de passage*). It acts as a substitute puberty rite. Our de-ritualized culture lacks ceremonial recognition of the transition from childhood to adulthood. Wearing the "permanent fade" gives ready-at-hand proof of growing up. The hickey ushers indecisive teenagers into adult sexuality as they imagine it. Negotiating it is a hurdle on the way to manhood or womanhood. The fleshy tattoo marks a significant developmental passage. It serves as a mini-rite or mini-ritual.

Growing Up: A Mini-Puberty Rite

Here come a few descriptions of how the hickey constitutes a developmental step.

- "I have partaken of the forbidden fruit of grownup sexual activity. I wear a badge to prove it to the world."
- "I discovered my sexuality slowly one step at a time and this hickey seemed to be another step that brought me closer to maturity."
- "My precious little hickey on his neck showed that I could make 'love-bites' just like adults."
- "Even though nobody else could see the fleshy tattoo on my breast, I knew the bite of male lust for me. I wasn't a little girl anymore!"

- "I wanted both to hide it from my parents out of shame but also to show it as part of my swagger of independence and rebellion."
- "My hickey marked the pain of growing up and the part sexual pains played in my process of maturing."
- "My hickey brought me to a 'crossroads'. Like the sketch of an arrow it pointed two ways: one reaching back to the roots of my raising and the other stretching to my future."

The Exhibits

The material of this book roots in my personal, professional, and daily life experience and my self-reflective search that transforms my experience to general meanings and ideas. In this section, I give a different type of evidence. An exhibit is the direct presentations of non-personal material from various sources and third-person witnesses. Any neutral, disinterested person can identify, examine, and corroborate documents, materials, testimonies, proofs, and externally created discussions. In contrast to 99.44% of what I present in this book, exhibits have nothing to do with my subjectivity or desire.

Exhibit A: Marks, Cuts, and Circumcision

Evidence exists that circumcision, the operation on the sex organ of both girls and boys is an ancient practice. Cultural agents used sharp pieces of flint before the use of a knife. Circumcision was a common place practice among the so-called primitive tribes of Africa, America, and Australia. It was unknown to the Indo-Europeans and Mongols. The popular mentality typically understood that medical concerns and hygienic considerations supported the practice. The chief intention, however, is a puberty rite. Circumcision initiates a child into adulthood most typically the young boy into manhood.

Among the Thonga tribe in South Africa the young boy undergoes six major trials in an elaborate ceremony to become a man. Every four or five years the group holds a "circumcision school." A boy who has reached the age of ten is sent to undergo severe "hazing" by the adult males.

> The initiation begins when each boy runs the gauntlet between two rows of men who beat him with clubs. At the end of this experience he is stripped of his clothes and his hair is cut. He is next met by e man covered with lion manes and seated upon a stone facing the "lion man." Someone then strikes him from behind and when he turns his head to see who has struck him his foreskin is seized and in two movements cut off by the "lion man." Afterwards he is secluded for three months in the "yard of mysteries" where he can be seen only by the initiated. It is especially taboo for a woman to approach these boys during their seclusion, and if a woman should glance at the leaves with which the circumcised covers his wounds and which form his only clothing, she must be killed (Whiting, Kluckhorn, and Anthony (1965/1958, 283).

Carmara Laye (1954/1964, 93) gives a sensitive portrayal of growing up in French West Africa. He describes what it is like to reach the "age of discretion," the time to "abandon childhood and my innocence, and become a man" through an essentially "secret tribal ceremony" which included the "dangerous ordeal . . . : circumcision."

> I wanted to be born, to be born again. I knew perfectly well that I was going to be hurt, but I wanted to be a man and it seemed to me that nothing could be too painful if, by enduring it, I was to come to man's estate. My companions felt the same; like myself, they were prepared to pay for with their blood. Our elders before us had paid for it thus; and those who were born after

us would pay for it in their turn. Why should we be spared? Life itself would spring from the shedding of our blood (Laye, 1954/1964, 94).

There is an inherent relationship between mutilation and circumcision. The Israelites, the people with whom the term circumcision has become synonymous, probably appropriated the practice from Egypt. We know from the evidence of the mummies that the Egyptians circumcised as early as the Old Kingdom. The Israelites, however, transformed the practice personally, culturally, and religiously. They only circumcised males. In addition to being a passage-rite it came to denote the basic difference between the Israelite and all other peoples, the gentiles who were uncircumcised. Circumcision signified the covenant indicating that Israel belonged to Yaweh, that God made the Israelites His chosen people. It also served as a seal of faith constantly reminding the people of the obligations of the convent.

By New Testament times, the ritual of circumcision took place eight days after birth. The child received his name. Simultaneously he became a member of the People of God, a participant in the messianic promise. St. Paul, spokesman for the new dispensation, argued in his Epistle to the Romans that circumcision as a concrete, physical act was superfluous. Forgiveness of sin and fulfilment of Yahweh's promise come through Baptism. He writes to the Colossians: "In him you have been circumcised, with a circumcision not performed by human hand, but by the complete stripping of your body of flesh. This is circumcision according to Christ."

The term has become metaphorical: the circumcision of the heart or spirit. The Catholic sacrament of confirmation has retained the multiple meanings of puberty rite and special belonging to the people of God. The bishop anoints the forehead of the boy/girl (near-puberty age) with chrism, an oil blessed at the Easter Vigil (itself a transformed Rite of Spring). The words of the confirmation rite are: "I sign thee with the sign of the cross, and I anoint you with the chrism of salvation . . ."

Exhibit B: Marks, tattoos, signs, brands and stigmata:

In the ancient Near East ownership of a slave was indicated by tattoo (στιγμα) placed on hand, wrist, or forehead. Pierced earlobes served a similar purpose. Runaway slaves and criminals were branded with fire on their foreheads in punishment. Eventually tattoos take on the religious significance of indicating a slave-like devotion to a god/goddess. In the New Testament St. Paul brags about the scars and scourges he had endured in his ministry in order to vouches for his fidelity to Christ. He boasts to the Galatians: "I bear the marks (στιγματα) of Jesus on my body."

A scar emblazoned with a seal of specialness, a stigma, pricked supernaturally later Christian mystics. Chesterton refers to St. Francis of Assisi's "mystical wounds" as indication that he mirrored Christ. He describes, imaginatively, the scene:

> The head if the solitary sank, amid that relaxation and quiet in which time can drift by with the sense of something ended and complete; and as he stared downwards, he saw the marks of nails in his own hands (Chesterton, 1957/1924, 131-32).

The Old Testament Book of Genesis records the "earliest" mark on the flesh, the original tattoo. Yahweh places a seal on Cain's forehead (= tattooed =stigmatized). The purpose is to display the brother-murderer crime and simultaneously to shield him against blood vengeance. Cain's tattoo was a typical tribal sign denoting punishment for a crime committed long ago. Such tattoos were frequently found among the Bedouins.

Dracula

I joke to family and friends that I am the only one who understands Dracula. "All he wanted was a kiss," I say, "and history has turned him into a sinister vampire." The truth in the joke is this. As most literary criticism, the corpus of literature about Bram Stoker's classic work is rationalistic. The touchstone of phenomena in human experience typically gets buried under layer after layer of theoretical analyses. So too, folklore about vampires—to which the hickey belongs—is rarely connected to raw life and to human experience. Myths, legends, fairy tales, folklore, and tall tales passed down from generation to generation always start with a human "moment." They are unlike what passes for contemporary fiction or the fantastic scripts of Hollywood blockbusters which are pure arbitrary concoctions, flights of fantasy used to entertain, to shock—to make money. They are not based in the register of the imagination which always works upon real life. Something happens; the imagination goes to work and hatches a story; and then the story takes on a life of its own. Whence, I ask, does a figure such as a vampire come to pass? It he or she just a product of abstract, arbitrary fancy? And unto today, are readers of *Dracula* and film goers merely curious about a figure that has no basis in human sensual experience? I think not.

Of course, nobody has the last word about the meaning of *Dracula* or of the Gothic novel. Arguably, it is a psychosexual allegory, probing the meaning of eroticism and its connection to love, blood, violence, and evil. In the chapters on the blush and kissing, I mention repeatedly the urge toward the blood of the sexual other. This yen for blood, what is it? It signifies the desire for "more." Again, repeatedly I have alluded to the "more" throughout this book. In our culture, "more" typically and almost exclusively means an accumulation of things or money. The "more" at stake in these sensual-sexual phenomena of loving is qualitative, not quantitative. It is what the soul wants, what the spirit craves, and what the heart aches for. In terms of the hickey, sucking the flesh awakens and stirs the blood of the beloved. Ron Cornelissen tells us that the hickey exposes the heart as being as vulnerable as the bruised skin: "I do not only suck the flesh of my beloved, I suck her heart. Blood takes a detour. The love-bruise leaves a heart's stain on the flesh. 'See, my love! You have my flesh; you have my blood; you have my heart'!"

I quote at length from Bram Stoker's novel (1897/1992) to exhibit the connection of the vampire to kissing and the hickey. Stoker introduces us early in his tale to three young women, "ladies by their dress and manner." Two were dark, and one was fair. Jonathan Harked, the protagonist, at first thought he was dreaming because the ladies did not cast a shadow. But they approached him, gazed directly at him, and whispered to each other.

> All three had brilliant white teeth that shone like pearls against the ruby of their voluptuous lips. There was something about them that made me uneasy, some longing and at the same time some deadly fear. I felt in my heart a wicked, burning desire that they would kiss me with those red lips (Stoker, 1897/1992, 46).

> The women whispered together and laughed.

> Such a silvery, musical laugh but as hard as though the sound never could have come through the softness of human lips. It was like an intolerable tingling sweetness of water glasses when played on by a cunning hand (Stoker, 1897/1992, 46).

They began to egg each other on to make contact with the protagonist. Jonathan's anticipation mounts when he hears one say, "He is young and strong; there are kisses for us all" (Stoker, 1897/1992, 46).

> The fair girl advanced and bent over me till I could feel the movement of her breath upon me. Sweet it was in one sense, honey sweet, and sent the same tingling through the nerves as her voice, but with a bitter underlying the sweet, a bitter offensiveness, as one smells in blood . . . The girl went on her knees, and

bent over me, simply gloating. There was a deliberate voluptuousness which was both thrilling and repulsive, and as she arched her neck she actually licked her lips like an animal, till I could see in the moonlight the moisture shinning on the scarlet lips and on the red tongue as it lapped the white sharp teeth. Lower and lower went her head as the lips went below the range of my mouth and chin and seemed about to fasten on my throat. Then she paused, and I could hear the churning of her tongue as it licked her teeth and lips, and could feel the hot breath on my neck. Then the skin of my throat began to tingle as one's flesh does when the hand that is to tickle it approaches nearer—nearer. I could feel the shivering touch of the lips on the super sensitive part of my throat, and the hard dents of two sharp teeth, just touching and pausing there. I closed my eyes in a languorous ecstasy and waited—waited with beating heart (Stoker, 1897/1992, 46-47).

The subject of an authentic psychology is not the ruling phenomena, cognition and behavior, but rather the passionate and tender soul and the heart with its warm blood. The rich folklore concerning vampires makes patently obvious existential facts about which what mainstream social science is ignorant. The kiss is either blessed or lethal. A hickey is a glorious badge or a hideous blot. A touch either brings a miracle to pass, or destroys.

CHAPTER FOURTEEN

The Caress:
The Miraculous Movement
of Tenderness

If there is a miracle or a magic touch, it is surely the caress. What is the difference between being "caressed" and being "pawed"? What does that difference reveal about sexual encounters? To address those questions I asked subjects to give a written response to this request "Based upon your own experience of being erotically touched, describe the differences between being 'caressed' and being 'pawed'.

Objective instruments, either a questionnaire, the measurement of galvanic skin responses, or film-data, are useless to show humanly related distinctions. They only record a transaction. The human subject who was touched alone can report its qualitative meaning. Only a woman could tell us that she felt 'manhandled' and that it made her flesh 'creep'. Only a man can say that getting 'jacked off' reduced his tension but made his skin 'crawl'.

Pawing is a 'hit-and-run' touch, the movement either of lust, need, pleasure, or thrill-seeking. For example: He grabs to 'cop a feel'; repulsed, she feels violated and infringed upon. "Let me *do* you, give you the best blow job you ever had," she boasts. She wants him to want her. "I'll get you off," he promises. He hopes to impress her with his sexual prowess and with his considerate attitude that she 'come' too. Pawing, crass and crude touching is the technique of seduction or manipulation.

Caressing is precisely the touch of *tenderness*. The sensible flesh communes with sensible flesh. It is *carnal intimacy* expressed by touching and fondling, with smell and taste, with squeezes and hugs, with nibbles and licks, by biting and sucking. My caress gives my beloved messages of largesse. It is my attempt at gift-giving or donation: "This is my body. With this body I love every part of *you*. Give *it* to me."

The caress is an ambiguous *double* of material and immaterial contact. Poets and songwriters wisely say that one feels on the inside a tender touch put outside on the skin. The hand that caresses is not reducible to muscles, bones, and nerves. It is not only an instrument, a tool, or a weapon. The hand that caresses is *my* hand. The fingers are *mine*. I have my hand in lots of ways. "This is my *loving* hand." When I gently stroke my beloved, softly rub her and probe, my actions express far better than mere words: "My heart is in my hands"; "This is my very soul"; or even "This is my entire life."

A caress is the body at play. It complacently enjoys the *carnal intimacy* of the nearness and accessibility of the beloved. I apply light friction against soft, smooth skin, silky hairs, and hot thighs; I rub more deeply the 'hard' organ or the 'moist' button at the delta. Skin against skin, locked in an embrace, chest to chest is voluptuous. It is the feeling of being at home. Nothing is more natural. Lovers swoon.

The caress searches blindly beyond the tangible, too. It grasps restlessly for an elusive feeling, reaching without knowledge or plans. The caress reaches for her who is always more than the body stretched out at my fingertips. It reaches for the person who is inexhaustible. Thus, the caress craves absence and seeks the "not yet." Fingers stretch and the hand aches for a future that cannot come quickly enough. Put slightly differently, the caress seizes upon *nothing*. It solicits what ceaselessly slips away (Levinas, 1961/1969, 257-258).

Under the caressing hand I am vulnerable and trusting. Surrender creates surprises, evokes unprecedented emotions, and brings an ordinary miracle to pass. "I never felt anything like this," he says, taking the words right out of her mouth. "You make me feel brand new," she says, before he might say it first. She asks, "How do you want this touch to end?" "I don't want it *ever* to end," he answers. "I want your touch to be first, last, and only."

The caress is also a *non-climatic* experience. Indeed, it never wants to end. I want another feel, one more rub, one more kiss, and then still another, and yet another. An intimate sex act does not *end* with climax. Orgasm does *not* put the finishing touch to the sexual moment. The lovely spasm, spurt, and little scream are equally the *beginning* of lovemaking. Lovers continue to cuddle, not wanting the moment done with. Then and there it would be "super fine" if the world came to an end! In the afterglow, they relish the prolonged embrace which is as much a part of the love making as the in-and-out twist and thrust.

"Sex is really only touch, the closest of all touch, D. H. Lawrence (1928/1983, 301) tells us, "and it is touch that we're afraid of." If the motive for sexual coupling is recreational sex or a one night stand, then the accent falls on skillful foreplay, proficient performance, and the pleasure exchanged. The curtain comes down quickly on the afterglow. Talk is meager: "Oh, good, you *came*." "Yeah, I got off." Or else it's: "I'm sorry I . . ." "Never mind, it doesn't matter . . . Next time . . . ." The act is some version of 'Wham-bam, thank you, madam'. Or she crows, "I *knew* you'd 'get off' on my body, betraying her self-aggrandizement. Sexual intercourse, lacking a tender caress and passionate embrace, decays into *cold-hearted fucking*.

What is pornography? Is it 'dirty' books, strip tease joints, lewd pin-ups, and XXX-rated videos? Is it not rather certain attitudes: that a male's body needs regular sex to "keep the pipes clean"; and that a woman's body needs periodic sex just as her piano keys tuned?

My fourteen year old male client, who was just discovering his sense of self, crowed jubilantly: "I luv me! I luv me! I wish there were two of me so that I could hang around with myself." The desire for reciprocity, mutuality, and sharing had not yet emerged in his scheme of things. Not surprisingly, he found her.

Risk-talk, contrariwise, trickles from the lips of intimate lovers: "I can't get enough of you." "I don't know *what* you're doing but don't stop." We hear words we can build a *love* upon. "I could die for the touch of a woman like thee" (Lawrence, 1928/1983, 135). We say words that we can build a *life* upon: "Almost anybody can have sex. No matter what we do we are making love all the time."

Concerning the power of touch between the genders, the classic description comes from the pen of D. H. Lawrence. I cull the following vignette from his literary masterpiece:

Lady Connie Chatterly and Mrs. Bolton are discussing the death of the latter woman's husband, twenty-three years earlier:

> One part of my life ended there. One part of me went with him . . . It was as if I could only feel his arms round me, an' his body against me, an' his legs against my legs . . . And I kept waking up thinking: "Why, he's not in bed with me" . . . . My feelings wouldn't believe he's gone. I felt he'd have to come back to lie against me, so I could feel him there with me, warm. And it took me a thousand shocks before I knew he wouldn't come back, it took me years . . . I've never got over the touch of him to this day and never shall. And if there's a heaven above he'll be there and will lie up against me so I can sleep' (Lawrence, 1928/1983, 175-176).

Concerning a man and a woman, Connie asks the basic existential question: "But can a touch last so long? . . . . Can a man's touch on a woman last so long . . . such that you still can still feel him?" The older woman gives the bedrock answer: "Eh, my Lady, what else is there to last? Children grow away from you. What else is there to last?"

"When he touches you?" Connie says.

"Yes, my lady, the touch of him" (Lawrence, 1928/83, 175-176).

CHAPTER FIFTEEN

Flirting Online: Cybersexuality[5]

Everything in life relates with everything else. Flesh and metal are twins not enemies. The living flesh and cyber-bodies swim together in the ocean of life, sometimes at odds with one another, sometimes synchronized, but never alone. To demonstrate the point, I describe an ordinary "moment" of daily life.

> My day breaks. It is still dark in Norway. I'm an early riser acquainted with the woes thereof. By habit I hit the button on the channel master; the Cable TV is on the blink this morning. I turned on my computer then slither into the kitchen. My espresso maker won't work. "Darn," I intonate and start brewing regular coffee. While my oatmeal is cooking, I try to go Online. The system is down. "Maybe my wireless isn't wired" I joke to myself. Squeezing in some honey, I nibble the piping hot oatmeal; it tastes like cut-off nails. Anyway, all is not lost: my cell phone is charging. I put down my spoon and check my SMS messages. There is only one: "I love you lots and lost." Immediately, I feel a chill crawling. Simultaneously, my nose smells my

---

[5]   Flirting on the Internet and the blush, the kiss, the hickey and the caress: A hermeneutic. Presented to the Fourth International Conference Cyperspace, Masyryk University, Brno, The Czech Republic, 24-25 November. 2006.

toast. Under my breath, I mutter. "Let her, uh, let it . . .
burn . . . in hell . . ."

I put on a CD. Too distracted or gutless to see which
disc I randomly fingered, I grab Vern Gosdin and
listen to him promise this night to do his damndest
not to drown in bourbon or tears. Now I am grinning
from ear to ear. With luck, the car will start. Hopefully,
Uncle Sam won't drop another atomic bomb today
on brown or yellow people. My Polish Grandmother
used to say, "When the truth hurts only a lie can be
beautiful." I've heard enough beautiful lies to last me
a lifetime. I start singing, two notes shy an octave, "If
technology doesn't kill me, your memory will."

Such is everyday life in postmodernity. We always had and
always will have technology with us. Gadgets escort our love.
Since touch touches everything, and we can't possibly give away
all our kisses or caresses, the coil of flesh and metal pervasively
twists, tangles, and unwinds our romantic lives. In fact we'd better
not "sleep in" lest while we doze someone furtively tries to FAX
us. Somewhere betwixt real life and cyberspace, we drift and soar,
stride and stumble, cuss and sing, laugh, dance, and wail. It's the
human condition. We are earthlings.

Flirting Online

Information technology continues to change the world. Today we
use I-Pods. I-Pads, and Smart Phones, do texting and blogging,
and enter Twitter, Facebook, Chat Rooms, and Blogspheres. Social
networking is changing the world by co-creating the Arab Spring
and Occupy Wall Street. People are meeting and acting in ways that
the Established Order cannot control. It is intoxicating. At least
half of us enjoy the sweet smell of freedom. At least half of us can
sing with Leonard Cohen that democracy is coming . . . And while
social media changes the socio-political landscape, it behooves

us to comprehend the lure and sway, the power and failure of cybersex. And it suits to interface love Online with love offline so that we might understand better and, therefore, make better choices in our sex life and love life and help our youth do the same. Let's call a spade a spade: Merely saying "No" never works.

Let us pop some questions: Why prefer a virtual mode to generate sexual attention? Why to gain and grant both social experience and romantic-erotic contact? Why choose the "chat" room as the arena for flirting? What happens after the "no holds barred" action is complete? What is the nature of the attachments that form in virtual reality? How do you start and how do you end?

Virtual Space

The chat room is tailor-made for flirting. One enters 'by "logging on" and chats by typing messages. At whim, any two users can move to a "private room" for one-on-one "talks." Since you can't "read" your partner's face, hear her voice, touch him, or smell her perfume, the sole medium of communication is textual "hot chat." Some users eventually do make phone calls, play with SMS, send email pictures, and even meet face-to-face.

Invisible Contact

In everyday social interaction, the main triggers of heterosexual interest are physical appearances, attractiveness, and /or meaningful talks about interests, attitudes, and values. These same spurs codetermine the perception of basic boundaries, co-define interpersonal situation, and motivate action within it. On the Net, however, a mental image stirs attraction. One develops that picture by reading and deciphering written texts. Also in daily life, the movement of social encounter hinge upon responses to the succession of steps. The Net offers no chance for the users to perceive each other's physical reactions. One must engage ceaselessly in the interpretation of written discourse.

Lisa used the chat room to build a serious virtual relationship with an American resident while she was living in northern Norway. She cultivated this contact during a "rough period." She and her "big love" had recently broken up. She had no desire to discuss her sorrow with friends. Because why? Well, with friends we share a history. Sit-down-drag-it-out-quasi-marathon-meetings demand time and effort. In such situations, most individuals minimally experience an implicit demand to take the other into consideration. Typically, two friends take mutual responsibility for each other. If your lover has "dumped" or "burned" you, a knit-picking, close-quartered *tête`a tête* exacts a high emotional cost. It can be suffocating. Such discussions exhaust Lisa. "Talking" to an anonymous individual can bear more fruit.

Lisa and her American male never met in the flesh. But they formed an "amazing link." Daily, they communicated by text, opening up to one another such to "became each other's best friend." At the start, Lisa had no intention to flirt or "play at love." Nevertheless, an emotionally intense man-woman "thing" developed.

How does Internet conversation facilitate such powerful attachments? The setting elicits projections of wishes, hopes, dreams, and fears. One attributes desirable or detestable characteristics to the ambiguous figure at the other end of cyberspace. You can fish for and garner satisfactions of both conscious and obscure needs. Meeting in the anonymity of cyberspace is a snap. With no density or heaviness, one readily opens up to a responsive other and "wings it." In the absence of threat, anonymity sets free.

Ending her offline romance with her first love was "heavy." Sharing physical space with anyone burdened her. In a word, she lost trust. With males she preferred "light" encounters over the Net, even "breezy" ones. A faceless, a-contextual engagement seemed perfect. She got "in touch" with someone with minimal exertion, and nourished the distant contact with the ease of just pecking keys. As soon as she communicated her intentions and received feedback, leaving-taking was at her fingertips. The chatting confirmed and healed her, costing nothing. Flirting, sometimes literally in the lengthening shadows of twilight or in pitch dark midnight, created daylight. Only the computer light was on. From her 'virtual' niche, she could disappear or impulsively "show off" and "shine." "It is important to see others and to be seen," Lisa tells. "In my lonely period, attentive acknowledgement mattered most." Faceless vision balanced her psychological economy.

What conditions make such virtual closeness possible? Text-based communication is ambiguously slow and, for the most part, unbelievably superficial. Small talk and sharing information at a 'snail's pace' . . . peck-peck-peck . . . facilitates gradually building a bond. To create something out of nothing demands repeatedly staining the blank, empty screen. Eventually, baring one's soul builds relationships as personal as face-to-face encounters, particularly along the dimensions of openness, risk, affection, receptivity, and trust. Whatever shape it assumes, consistent, reliable, sustained contact is nothing to sneeze about.

John, the other participant-subject, always skeptical about Internet dynamics, kept his virtual involvements superficial. He just "played." He never gave out his phone number or home address, and never attempted sustained contacts. For him "serious flirting is a face-to-face affair."

Netspeak

Human communication is always ambiguous. Whether we are writing a letter, shouting face-to-face, or whispering in the dark, we never catch all nuances. Something always gets lost in "translation." Typically, we protest: "You took that the wrong way." Whenever we make a "slip" in speech or in writing, demonstrating conflicted intentions, then the whole kit and caboodle goes up for grabs.

Body language in the social arena helps us to decipher ambiguous man-woman communication. Although Netspeak is by text only, still Internet interaction does not totally obliterate the communicant's non-verbal channels of gesture, posture, tone of voice, rate of speech, and volume. A special language has evolved whereby users of electronic media insert non-verbal messages into their texts via symbols and abbreviation. Emoticons convey special and detailed feelings, e.g., a face to show that you are smiling :) or frowning (: or an expression such as *lol* that means "laughing out loud." This stylized and staccato language is similar to adolescent jargon (classic "pig" Latin) and to Western society's obsessive use of hackneyed initials that only makes sense to those within the in-group familiar with the code.

Online users become editors, punctuating texts with nuanced responses that aim to minimize ambiguity and banish ambivalence. Users, plopped in front of a screen, try to clarify expressions of sarcasm and irony, just as do writers of traditional letters . . . or two intimates standing in front of each other, wagging tongues.

Arousal-by-Text

Online flirting often triggers physical and sexual reactions stronger than in a regular conversation: shuddering, shivering, having an erection, and blotching. In an existential situation, a compliment or tease might provoke a blush that glares like a neon light. Over the net, one shares the heat and reddening by using brackets: (blush). Thus, moment-by-moment punctuations diminish the gap between the screen and the Lifeworld. John insists that the special slang of Internet dialogue is "more direct" than most "oral" interactions.

What's the line of demarcation between "chatting" and "flirting?" As in any business office or tavern, it is subtle. Consciously or not, one goes either to a disco or Online with motives and for a purpose. Someone has to take initiative for "it" to happen. In a "chat room," one party must click twice on the other's name so that they can meet alone in a "private room" where no one can follow their conversation. As is true in the marketplace and workplace, privacy activates a powerful dynamism. Hidden conversations, secret meetings, and clandestine actions are "Outlaw" fodder that spontaneously quicken the risk to court the exciting "stranger."

By making the first 'click', one sets the mood and often decides immediately to orchestrate an obvious flirt, or else settle for another run-of-the-mill "rap." The other participant either follows the lead, or switches focus, or terminates the session. Click!

No standard exists for developing the conversation. Most participants start respectfully, with polite questions and gentle invitations. Some players, without any lead-in, do pose direct questions of an intimate character. Knowledge of the slang, as the case with any language, facilitates swift and early detection of the other's motives and intentions. It also minimizes possible bruises to sensibilities that "rough" chat room tactics can inflict. To refuse your correspondent's invitations, one can easily log off. Click!

The snail's pace of text-based communication especially facilitates the gradual development of a long-term bond. Likewise, the direct style and focused jargon of cyberspace fosters "recreational flirting" and the rapid emergence of pseudo-intimacy. Most users are not geeks, freaks, or weirdoes. They just use a ready-to-hand tool to make contact. In most normative social situations, says John, "You can't say some things to people the first time you meet them. But you can say anything immediately over the Net."

John predicts that people will increasingly take advantage of the unfettered format. Society bulges with rules and norms about social conduct. Until familiarity develops between the genders, typically reserve marks encounters in public places. But on the information highway, there are no "red lights." Cyberspace grants a free breath of fresh air. Nothing stops you from revealing your innermost desires and wildest imaginings. If your yen is a one-in-a-row sexually oriented conversation . . . with a specific erotic outcome in mind . . . or on your body . . . then you can easily toss politeness and caution to the four winds. Sometimes the winds bellow . . . and wildly rage.

Imagination or Fantasy?

Sexually-romantically tinged fantasies fuel flesh and blood encounters. But the inherent structure of sensory deprivation in cyberspace maximally fires the imagination. Basic facts about the other's looks, color, or length of the hair, or of height or weight, are like so many Rorschach ink blot cards. One concocts an image out of the ambiguous blots that may or may not correspond to the co-respondent's actual physiognomy.

Concerning their forays into cyberspace, both Lisa and John sharply distinguish between imagination and fantasy. In the absence of visual cues, imagination necessarily fills the blanks. Although John did not admit engaging in cybersex with Online partners, he had sexual fantasies about some and considers the imagination important to flirting. He was "in the game to explore and experiment, open to have fun and take whatever opportunity the situation might give." He adds, "You exaggerate a little . . . imagining you can successfully 'hit' on the woman. It's more fun that way." But he kept him imagination to himself. Lisa denies having sexual fantasies about her Net correspondents, but says, "I did imagine the people I met and got to know."

In virtual politics, however, fantasy is the key strategic tool. If the participants wish cybersex, they quickly mention what "turns them on." They graphically describe what they are just then doing with their own bodies, or what they fantasize doing with the other's body. The lonely solo flight of masturbation soon doubles into the dubious pleasure of mutual masturbation.

Who's the Other?

A cyber-interaction differs qualitatively depending upon whether the partner is a new acquaintance or someone with whom you already have bonded. Intimate partners, temporarily separated, experience email as a distance-shrinking lifeline. Your heart skips a beat when the electric voice chimes, "You've got mail!" The text functions as substitute 'touch'. Cybersex with an imperfect stranger, however, lacks a shared carnal or intimate history.

What Makes Sex . . . . Sex?

Thorny questions emerge. What is the meaning of sexual gratification over the net? Is it sex? Doubtlessly, cybersex grants temporary release, some tension-reduction, plus the additional pleasure of thinking that your correspondent co-generates and shares your excitement. Virtual sex fills a lack. But Robin Hamman (1996) muddies the water concerning the quality of the fulfillment: "I feel angered and cheated at the possibility that it is not the others in cyberspace that have done these things to me, but my fantasies." It boils down to, "I am masturbating myself . . . in the absence . . . of your presence. Are you masturbating too, alone, in my absent . . . presence?" After touching the mouse . . . no more 'pop ups' flash on the screen . . . which darkens . . . or the stars turn blue . . . then it gets lonesome, empty, and cold.

Until today, Lisa is unsure. Was her "best friend and cyber-lover" 'toying' with her from the get-go? In cyberspace, one never knows. Interpreting Internet discourse is an ambiguous labor. We do get duped face-to-face, too, but with more opportunity to push for truth. Eyeball-to-eyeball dialogue is infinite. The last word is never spoken. The other can always say "No!" or open the conversation anew. The last word, on the Net, is just a (: away. Click!

Fantasy versus Meeting

Lisa got more than she bargained for while seeking temporary respite in cyberspace. She still prefers cultivating long-lasting relationships. For her, the natural progression is to initiate contact, flirt, develop a relationship, and then meet. Will the person correspond to one's fantasies? Finding out requires risk. When Lisa drummed up courage to lay eyeballs on one guy, she found him totally opposite to the way he "came off" on the screen. She concludes from experience most guys are "one person on the net, another, different one in real life."

John experienced the same split. A telephone conversation with his Online partner "shocked" him. The pitch and dialect of the girl's voice turned him off. It failed to match how his imagination construed her textual messages.

Simulation

Will the picture fit the words? The question haunts cyberspace. Unless you eventually lay eyes on the naked visage, no answer comes forth. A flesh and blood encounter may either pleasantly surprise or devastatingly disappoint you. For every tale of finding a soul-mate, marrying, and riding off into the sunset a corresponding story documents love gone "wrong." Trivial but important factors matter. One simply did not like the way a guy smells; or when she put her tongue in your mouth it felt so thick you gagged as if you had swallowed an eel.

The Ambiguity of Cyberspace

The tension about the fit between the 'author' of texts and the 'actor' in life plagues regular and infrequent users alike. The virtual forum allows you to shape the situation to fit your own whim. In cyberspace, there are no limits, no boundaries, no rules, regulations, no traffic signals . . . and no border-crossings. You can interpret the other's initiative such that it thrills you, attributing qualities and virtues that set your head a-spinning. You can shape any preferred self-portrait and even create as many identities as you wish by using a program called an IRC (Internet Relay Chat). Just logon, develop "profiles," confabulate, and rehearse roles.

The strong lure to hide safely behind the computer screen tempts most users. You orchestrate the "music," direct the "play," and juggle several personalities. John affirms, "Only your own moral standards and feelings set the limits. Literally, it is "heady control".

The terrifying moment, to repeat, comes whenever two users decide to meet in the existential forum. Push then comes to shove. Lisa nails the 'moment': "You risk getting answers that rattle you brain and tug at your heart. You find out that imagination and reality do not square. Something dies."

Reflections on Online Flirting and Eye-to-Eye Carnal Contact

Online, one orchestrates cyber-romances or virtual sex *in safety*, sitting *alone* facing a brightly lit screen with hand on mouse. With seeming ease, users—youngsters in particular—cope with issues that had plagued their "modern" counterparts: shyness, pressure to act sexual, fear of rejection, and the strain of forming a relationship. Cybersex is "clean," less pressure-riddled and easier to negotiate than intensely emotionally-laden interactions in real life (RL). Presented with a disturbing message Online, or faced with a sudden threat, a user simply logs off. Equally simply, she can log on later after having considered her response and gotten her bearings. Of course, the technological doors are ever open for cyber-bullying and cyber-stalking. But that is another long story for another research project.

Strategies and plans, aims and objectives, thoroughly simulated, *modulated* and thick with **control** bloat Online practices. If one craves safety and security in romantic entanglements, bet on screen encounters. Before anything can get too far out of hand, one exercises the power to control the "drift" with a smile or maybe a sneer. Or a click!

The hickey again! On the other hand, nobody possesses a recipe for exchanging hickeys. While facing another bodily, the power to control is tenuous. A pause generates nothing. If you blink or hesitate, that's when jaws are apt to snap in a wanton bite. Standing or lying face-to-face, one is raw, exposed and maybe naked. There is no easy exit. When you least expect it, out of the blue comes . . . a touch, a kiss, a hickey.

The hickey is a spontaneous maverick, a flagrant mark that resists the reduction of sexuality to a series of self-referential signs. The simple itch foils simulated and mediated sex. Literally, you can't get out of your skin! I repeat: *you can't get a hickey over the Internet.*

Some individuals find exciting computer contact; but it bores others to tears. "Mouth-sucking-skin" thrills one person; another finds it childish, unsanitary, or disgusting. Because why? Although throughout this book I have tried to minimize theoretical word-spew, in this regard three theoreticians have relevant thoughts to contribute. John Money's "lovemaps" (1986), Jacques Lacan's "mirror enchantment" (1949/1977) and Emmanuel Levinas' phenomenology of the face (1961/1969; 1975/1996) provide frameworks for understanding the two varieties of arousal.

Similarities between the Two Styles of Flirting

From the perspective of John Money, hickey and Online comportment share the common fibre of being subgroups of the same *lovemap*. Money says we are all equipped with a template for sexual attraction, a map as natural as our body and brain. None fall in love without one. One's peculiar lovemap, not innate or in-born, begins at an early age and gradually differentiates like a native language. Links forged as early as age eight can last a lifetime.

Map-images are both *idealized* and as uniquely *individualized* as fingerprints. They depict one's perfect lover and interaction in an idealized, romantic, erotic and sexualized relationship. The popular idiom has it that "love is blind." The blindness stems from our tendency to project our map-image. The ensuing disappointment is an index of how rarely our image of our heartthrob squares with other peoples' perception. Likewise, Money (1986) explains Online attraction by the dynamics of the "loveblot," i.e., the mutual projection and "wearing" of a map.

Online users and traders in hickeys exemplify the lovemap of *solicitation and allure*. That map includes conveying sexuoerotic arousal by displaying and watching, touching and rubbing, talking or listening, and writing or reading. A description of two versions of the map explicates the similarities and differences. To make his point, Money uses awkward words that he concocts from the Greek tongue.

Stigmatophilia (The love of marks)

The hickey, of course, exemplifies one version of this map, stigmatophilia. Sexual arousal is triggered by "tattooing, scarring, and piercing the body . . . the practice of having markings branded, pricked, cut, or pierced into the body, especially into its erotic regions. Tattooing the genitalia and piercing the perineum, genitals, or nipples enables one to wear gold bars, rings, or chastity locks and use them for erotic allure . . . The macho lure of tattoos and pierced gold genital jewelry or earrings is often favored by those whose erotic uniforms comprises high boots with chains and spurs, studded leather jackets, pants and wristbands, leather cockstraps, and other macho paraphernalia."

Narratophilia (The Love of Texts)

Textual flirting typifies the other type of solicitation: "genitoerotical arousal by telling, listening to or reading graphic erotic texts, tales or stories . . . 'dirty' talk that rouses us and/or to sustains excitement" (Money, 1986). The verbal solicitation of Net-speak, however, or the invitation to touch and bite would fail to arouse individuals equipped with a different lovemap, e.g., "sacrifice and expiation," "marauding and predation," mercantile and venal strategies" (Money, 1986).

Differences between the Two Styles of Flirting

Three theories clarify the sharp differences between the two styles. Lacan's notion of "mirror enchantment" reveals the roots of the incredible seductive power of imaginary "screen" eroticism; and Levinas demonstrates the primacy of the eyes and of touch.

Mirroring

Lacan's (1949/1977) seminal idea is the "mirror stage." A six month old, presented in the mirror by mother or father, squeals with joy in a moment of self-recognition and bodily wholeness. But it's a moment of alienation too. The parent is crowing with enthusiasm and talking up a storm! The baby assumes the parents' glee as if her very own Thus the mirror reflects back both the personal *je* and the objectified *moi*. The entrapment is dynamic: she puts the image on! Henceforth, it will transfix her. Captured in the mirror, incessantly, addictively, she will seek to re-evoke that original jubilant instant . . . will identify as 'love' whatever triggers the same pleasure . . . will be raw with misery—suicidal even—when the pleasure fails or fades . . . and will become adept at projecting "it" onto the least likely of "texts." Even if pleasure (*plaisier*) does spontaneously surface, her task will be to decipher if it is her own satisfaction (*jouissance*) or merely the pleasure of the other.

Since time immemorial, imaginary gratification has swallowed up sexuality. Nobody ever bragged that isolated pleasure—with a book, magazine, a photo, or a memory—was life's ultimate satisfaction. Today's virtual forms of play, albeit often supremely serious, do not inscribe a full life. Whenever someone gets trapped in a hall of mirrors, addicted to a screen-life or erotically entangled in the Net, there is no reason to applaud the disturbance.

Lacan's thinking clarifies a cardinal point of this paper. Over the net, 'no body' does not equal 'no presence'. Within the register of the imaginary, absence is a mode of poignantly powerful presence that intensifies lustful urges and passion. This entire book does not pivot around embodiment in the superficial, behavioral sense. It cuts into the problem of embodiment at ground level, revealing Western ideology as life-denying, flesh-degrading and earth-demeaning (Nietzsche, 1883/1982).

Richard J. Alapack

Equivocal vulnerability and exorbitant materiality

The Face

Levinas' (1961/1969 basic word is "The eyes do not shine, they speak." Concerning Eros, he makes a revolutionary move. He melds into one comprehensive gestalt the whole person: the frankness of the naked visage, the caress of trembling hand, the bareness of the exposed body, the denuding of the sexual pair, and risk-talk. Thus, he elaborates and amplifies what Freud means by *schaulust*, desire that emerges from looking. From Levinas' perspective, virtual interactions offer half-messages which erode the flowing adhesiveness of paying a face-to-face visit, the natural rhythms of chatter and touch, eye-talk and body-speak. Online discourse, therefore, only fits rational, secondary relationships. Intimacy requires the full spectrum of the vital sensing feeling.

Eyes/No Eyes

A theme throughout this book, starting with peekaboo, is the link between vision and splendor. The eyes are carnal and erotic. The shared look between an individual and an-other or a gallery of others is the necessary condition for the blush even to occur, and it is pivotal for the meaning of the hickey. The eyes talk. There are distinct qualitative differences in the meaning of "sexuality" between what happens in the encounters that trigger blushing or the hickey and what transpires over the Net.

Eyes talk. Absence of eyes also talks. The perception of naked flesh is possible. The two are in reach of each other, a fingertip away from the magic of touch. They are in eye-sight. The possibilities of looking and touching energize the situation in a particular way. Thus, the phenomena of modesty, averting the eyes, and blushing are sexual. Kierkegaard (1844/1980, 68-69) even insists that there is "no temptation as fascinating as that of modesty." When a shared fleshy look is not even possible, then although something definitely transpires across the wires, it is sex-in-the-head, imaginary sexuality. It lacks the vulnerability, the challenges, and the risks of face-to-face, back-to-back, belly-to-belly encounters. "Momentary" red hot passion ceases at the touch of a mouse. As mentioned above, one wonders if the pleasure traded is not just a variant form of masturbation. Technosexuality is a substitute for fleshy sexuality, a simulated form. As such, it satisfies our societal clamor for safe sex. They also unmask this political tactic as hypocritical: 'Safe sex is an oxymoron. Cybersex is only safe because it is 'no-sex' (Alapack, Flydal Blichfeldt and Elden, 2005, 60). The Internet is a giant condom that shrouds carnal sensuality-sexuality, not just preventing but controlling it.

Control is the core reason for the Establishment's support of Information Technology. Under the ruse of building an information highway, the Net is the quintessential Panopticon (i.e., the structure for surveillance and social control). In the everyday Lifeworld, it is hard to say "No" to a sexual invitation while poised eyeball-to-eyeball and belly-to-belly. The spontaneous "moment"readily paves the way for the transmission of sexual diseases. But all the "Yesses" in the world during phone sex will never lead to AIDS. Such control gives a whole new meaning to the phrase, "Smart Phone."

Carnal desire has always befuddled normal science and technology. They simply cannot incorporate into their models the spontaneous blaze of hot flesh. One blushes beet red, then the glow subsides; no mechanical gadget can harness this heat. A caress melts you, and you swoon; how can we index this liquid? Someone 'paws' you and your skin creeps; no technical apparatus exists to capture this shudder. Carnal desire cuts. Fingernails dig into flesh, scratch and mar it, drawing blood. The bite breaks the skin and bruises it. The hickey hurts. Trading a hickey is like firing a carnal-engine and triggering a mini-revolution. The flow of unleashed desire gives blatant evidence that 'bruised skin' is of a different order than a 'bruised ego'. At root, the excesses of marks and stains are dangerous. *The hickey threatens the established social order.* Cybersex, on the other hand, easily fits into machinery. It is fruitless to expect a research grant to study the hickey, but cybersex is a multi-million dollar industry.

CHAPTER SIXTEEN

Fashion

Zones of sensual and sexual lure open up and close in an intimate link with popular culture. Fashion, like visual media and music, is an ever-present pivot around which swings this two-way door. Consequently, although the preferences of fashion to reveal or conceal certain bodily regions are transitory, they are never trivial. Each passing fad, as it lingers and fades, pinpoints the crux of its historical moment and thus bears theoretical significance. It is especially the young who are most vulnerable and most affected by the power of these shifting trends. Insofar as fashion interweaves wardrobe and skin, makeup and hairstyles, perfume, jewelry and accessories, it mediates the shifting winds of social climate.

Maurice Merleau-Ponty demonstrates that the human body is not only an *object* of observation, but also a meaning-creating *subject* and a *medium of culture*. Clothing does not just drape the flesh, but extends it. Clothing reveals personal ambitions, social aspirations and the spirit of the times. One stellar way to espy the waxing, waning and displacement of *political power* is to pay attention to what adolescent girls and women are wearing.

Arguably, ours is an anorexic-bulimic culture. Slimness as a feminine ideal co-constitutes the pressing problem of eating disorders. Although commercials promoting gluttony bombard the American public, nevertheless the main mission of the System nowadays is to eliminate obesity—especially since an increasing number of American children are "living extra-large." In alarming rates, however, more and more youngsters are starving themselves. Gluttony jostles with obesity which collides with starvation! In order to make sense out of these warped attitudes to eating, we must understand the relationship between adolescent identity and fashion, and unravel the strands that tie fashion to psycho-social-political-historical matters.

In each segment of history, fashion singles out some section of the female skin as sensuous. Despite incessant disclaimers, the advertising, entertainment, cosmetic, diet, fitness, and tanning industries massively exploit the female face and torso. Unconscionably, the medical profession colludes with this exploitation. Under the guise of health care, it pushes weight-control pills and authorizes a plethora of radical body "make-over" procedures, bodily replacements and prosthetics, plastic and/or weight-reduction surgery. The next chapter will discuss in detail this "siege."

Erotic images also continuously flood the Internet, glut our billboards, newspapers magazines, and cloy the pre-previews at the Cineplex. Largely because of the popularity of "reality" television, explicit eroticism so surfeits so-called 'prime time' that the medium has drifted towards "soft porn." Cable TV perennially exacts high subscription fees because it offers for consumption a smorgasbord of "meat." Hollywood has long promoted the multi-billion dollar pornography industry.

Cover girls posing and models parading before our eyes are usually attractive, mostly young or young looking, typically thin, and either scantily or provocatively clad. Democratic-capitalism, in its insatiable quest to open new markets, demands for its 'sell' sexual signifiers and prefers that female flesh should be . . . accessible. Since the almighty dollar coaches this "skin" game, planned obsolescence marks the garment industry. In principle and in fact, relentless *change* rules fashion. Frequently must switch the fleshy feminine *location* that *t*emporarily is chic to show nude. Within this flux of "floating signifiers," a subtle dialectic sustains between the *mode of apparel* and the *dominant social paradigm* (Baudrillard, 1988). Sometimes, prevailing mores shift such as happened during the socially radical 1960s when fashion went tie-dyed and bra-less. At other times, fashion itself triggers attitudinal changes, like when Madonna made fashionable wearing her undergarments on the outside. The "moment" for baring certain bodily zones is an eye-blink.

Reasons for paradigmatic changes concerning body disclosure are never accidental. During the 20th century, first breasts and then legs constituted the lure of fashion and the bait of commerce. A dramatic shift took place as we were about to collide with the millennium. New styles displayed zones of female anatomy typically concealed during modernity. As usual, the radical modes emerged first on the runway and at gala events which showcase pop stars, actors, musicians, and so-called celebrities. Eventually, a raging popular fad emerged that exposed the stomach, belly button, and crack of the ass. Various labels designate this trend: the bare bellybutton look; the butt-cracked chic; the visible G-sting syndrome; the ass-flash; the open waistband look and the visible underwear style. Each of these interchangeable labels depicts one aspect of an identifiable gestalt: **the epiphany of flesh and skin.**

Etymologically, epiphany means *manifestation* or showing. This style indeed ex-poses bare flesh so flagrantly graphically and starkly brazenly that it radically recodes rules regarding the visual representation of feminine flesh. It affords bodily assets and flaws no place to hide. Consequently, it shifted the paradigm.

The style, for example, makes bodyart imperative. The female encircles her mid-rift with a gold chain and usually pierces her tummy with a golden ring, a diamond stud or a less expensive jewel. She decorates, too, the prominently exposed small of her back with a tattoo—a simple sun or a more intricate peacock. She even adorns with tattoos or jewelry, intimate bodily spots heretofore "unmentionable" in public. The look does not just wrap a woman in clothes and adorn her with jewelry, but converts her body into an open canvas of bare skin, vividly, colorfully, and even expensively ornamented. Such explicitness faces men and women in our patriarchy with the power of the **pearl** and the **hole**. This essay probes the meaning of this confrontation. It also places it within a psycho-social-politico-historical perspective insofar as it is a class phenomenon, as conspicuously present among the privileged elite as it is absent from among the poor and destitute.

Dennis Hall (2005) describes four clothing tactics or strategies of body disclosure that coalesce to form this style, 1)Turning underwear into outerwear; 2) Exposing skin ordinarily covered when dressed, e.g., "plunging necklines, bare midriffs, skirts slit to the thigh, extremely short skirts, open waist bands, unbuttoned blouses, dresses with revealing cutouts and thong underwear"; 3) Diaphany, i.e., the use of transparent materials and fabrics, so fine of texture as to permit seeing through them; 4) Liquefaction, i.e., the use of opaque fabrics so fine and pliable that they cling to the body of the wearer as if a second layer of skin. While still covering flesh, they reveal thereby every contour and even the texture of the woman's body, looking as if poured upon the wearer, e.g., "clothes made of fishscale and fine, metallic knits, Lycra, spandex, rayon or silk jersey or ultra-fine closely fit knits."

The wax and wane of this visible underwear style is also pertinent. In the spring of 2001, very young teenagers exhibited the upper line of their panties against the open midsection. At prom time in June, American high school students wore gowns cut low in the back, narrowing to a V-cut, plunging below the small of the back to the tattooed tailbone. By summer 2002, the style had reached its zenith of popularity. The garment industry foisted it on the female population at large. Many women complained that shops and boutiques only stocked cropped blouses and shirts and low-riding jeans. Willing females took advantage of the risqué garments to flaunt their 'hard bodies' and, by leaning forward while bra-less, offered a provocative view of what slang calls "hooters."

As autumn approached, journalist Olivia Baker coined the "Brittany effect," alleging that trendsetting starlets like Ms. Spears, Mariah Carey and Jennifer Lopez were creating mother-daughter "back-to-school battles." Baker (2002) poses provocative mock questions: "Does Brittany's racy style have a bad influence on young girls?"; "Would you let your daughter dress like Brittany?"

In effect, such media spin served as a *commercial* insuring that for another season or two the style would remain mainstream attire. It only began to wane in the summer of 2003, after the illegal USA invasion of Iraq and the start of its occupation. Following the 2 November 2004 Presidential election, it became passé. Hollywood's Academy Awards Show on 28 February 2005 dramatically exhibited the fade out. Ella Taylor (2005) mocked Oscar award winner Hilary Swank's gown—a backless, ruched, high-necked and long-sleeved Guy Laroche design—as "a pneumatically enhanced Speedo with a fish tail and a get-thee-to-a-nunnery front." The apparel at "Oscar at 77" definitely eschewed any raunchy exposure of flesh.

The spring 2005 fashions also spurned outrageously porous designs, shocking shades, and bold patterns. The new arrivals featured subtle sophistication in the form of classically tailored jackets, romantically pretty dresses, neat black pencil skirts, and pastel shaded skirts finished with a gentle sheen and embellished with delicate metallic embroidery. Mirroring the ultra-conservative choice made by fifty-nine million USA voters, fashion harkened back to blatant *cover-up*.

These conservative styles parade as major values secrecy, security, and the right-winged Christian dread of raw flesh and condemnation of unbridled sensuality. Long gypsy skirts, worn with a belt as an accessory, drape the *truth* of the flesh as do pleated skirts, accompanied by a cardigan sweater. The tastefully chic short skirts are demure, not racy. Pretty tunic tops hide the torso from neck to below the mid-drift. Cropped slacks and trousers expose just the woman's ankle—minimally seductive no matter how nicely turned. With the return of the Empire style in the summer 2005, the waist of dresses *migrates from just above the hips to just below the solar plexus*. Ads crows that its conservative design "flatters your *curves* and creates a shapely *silhouette* while simultaneously draping the navel. Empire waists haven't been this popular since Napoleon set up housekeeping on Elba" (*MSN*, 2005). Within a six-year span, styles had flip-flopped 180 degrees. By the time Hurricane Katrina hit, the radical shift to reactionary clothing was complete. Such unblushing epiphany followed by severe veiling requires interpretive probing. What are the psycho-social-political meanings?

Firstly, what makes the clothes of the belly button look flattering and the butt-crack chic appealing? What is the logic of the lure? Ronald Bathes (1991, 9-10) describes the sexual triggers: "Is not the most erotic portion of the body *where the garment gapes*? The *intermittence* is erotic . . . skin flashing between two articles of clothing . . . this *flash* is erotic, the staging of appearance-as-disappearance and disappearance-soon-to-reappear." Once again, this is an alternate statement of what Freud means by the lustful look, *schaulust*. The voluptuous look is part and parcel of the lure of all fashion.

Spring Snow exemplifies the basic structure of such lure. The young protagonist, Kiyoaki, "reels" in the face of Princess Kasuga's "dazzling burst of elegance . . . a great fan of white fur a-glow fading to the sound of music, like a *snow-covered peak first hidden then exposed by the fluid pattern of clouds*" (Mishima, 1973, 6-7).

Put more prosaically, the look transforms a woman's body into a pattern-in-flux. The design of her outer garments allows every move to veil or unveil some patch of skin and/or undergarment. It adorns her body in skimpy, slashed, or perforated garments visible behind beads, transparent veils, and translucent scarves. Partially naked skin plays peek-a-boo with the eyes of the beholder; flirting, teasing, and tantalizing even while camouflaged under "flesh colored nipple covers." Low-rise jeans, cut low at the hips and loosely hanging, combine with a short scanty crop-top blouse or shirt to expose the waist. Eventually, the designers so layer the garments that multiple flimsy pieces move and slide, as if pulled by an unseen pulley.

The "flash" hallmarks the style. Jeans slide downwards, forcing sheer panties to pop up. Skin and garment flip flop in oblique views and undulating vistas: white panties gleam against brown skin; black bikini briefs glisten against patches of light flesh. Every gesture and movement creates a new configuration. The female stretches: the cut-off shirt lifts to reveal her midsection, ribs, and upper torso. She tugs her jeans and her panties recede from view. As soon as she lets go, the garment drops again and uncovers sheer thongs. Whenever she stretches forward, the action reveals her string-bikinis and the top tip of the crack of her butt. As soon as she straightens up, the panties disappear again. Simultaneously, her blouse inches up close to her breast line.

Shannon Rupp (2004) calls this short lived outburst and constantly shifting manifestation of skin the "ass-flash," and accents the accompanying "bared naughty bits and décolletage-cut-to-the-crouch." This epiphany style choreographs a carnival of sensual flesh, hidden then exposed: a merry-go-round of transient erotic scenes, skin covered and soon shown bare; a Ferris wheel of looks, round and around; a tilt-a-whirl of peeks, up and down. A mole shows and then vanishes; freckles wonderfully spread out before the eyes; a beauty mark appears then recedes from view. Each female is an *active architect* of a panorama in flux. Her choice in undergarments, the way she decorates her body, and her choice of movements, controls how much of her skin or undergarments show. No other style in the history of fashion 'forces' such choices upon a woman; none affords power to influence the impact of her attire upon a man insofar as, moment to moment, she rearranges her total appearance.

Interpreting the Bare Belly Look

This *intermittent flashing* harbors a meta-message. Does not the fashion industry shrewdly promote sensuality by highlighting equally the *seen* and the *unseen*? The visible and invisible form a unified picture. The hackneyed explanation for this practice is that fashion must leave as much to the imagination as it grants to the eyes. However, that view is shallow. Interpretation yields a richer understanding of erotic perception. Pinpointing any single bodily part as an erogenous zone is foolish (Barthes 1991). Sigmund Freud (1905) writes that the entire human body is "polymorphous perverse" or the opposite of repressive neurotic pathology. Sensuality is co-created. It erupts spontaneously, but simultaneously something summons it forth. The epiphany style solicits it by orchestrating the vacillation of the appearance and disappearance of skin. The eye gazes and then focuses. One erotic flash follows another. Each compels vision in a different way.

The Patriarchy: Under Assault or Perpetuated?

Does this maximization of both intermittence and flash finally usher in a historical "moment" of genuine womanly power? A minority of females do wear the look with ease. Some carry it with such pizzazz that the onlooker would swear either they invented it or someone tailored it especially for them. They revel in the half-nude look which displays their 'assets': ivory smooth skin, a lovely bellybutton, or a 'hard body' with flat, sculpted, washer-board tummies—the result of endless hours of 'abs' exercises. Under an appraising gaze, their physiognomies ooze confidence and radiate grace. Men *notice; they notice . . . men noticing . . .*

Nevertheless, not all females who buy the clothes wear them comfortably or with confidence. Some women look odd in them. The full-figured "Queen" sized woman cannot gracefully display her stomach, belly button, or derriere. Carrying a proverbial "spare tire" around her "rim," she cannot don flimsy, porous garments. If she fails to match the various garments with finesses, on her the look looks ridiculous. Some women that try to dress in the style seem clueless about the effect their appearance has on appraising males. Suppose a woman, instead of donning risqué briefs under low-rise trousers, wears ample bloomers—Costco all-cotton fullbacks. When she bends to pick up her infant from its carriage, her flashing droopy drawers look ludicrous. Said bluntly, the epiphany style displays graceful sleek women, not thick hips and rolls of flesh. Not surprisingly, while the style was 'hot' more than a few ladies—especially obese Americans—never adopted it and could not wait for it to die out. They *notice . . .* that men *do **not** notice them . . . but even look away.*

Whether or not a woman prefers the exposed mid-section look, few wear it in a relaxed manner. To protect their bodily comfort-zone, even those who wear it with confidence fuss with it. Bracket momentarily the relaxed comportment of professional G-string divas, prancing on cue, dancing the hip-hop on MTV, strutting down the runway, or performing with flair under lights and cameras! In everyday life, few women fail to fiddle with the short skimpy garments. While exiting a bus, restlessly they pull down their cropped top to cover their navels; whenever greeting a room full of people, they pull up low-riding jeans to cover exposed underwear. At a less than conscious level, they are vigilant not to exhibit too much skin, especially while engaged in a task like getting out of an automobile or handling objects that require much movement or make them have their "hands" full—such as pumping gas at the service station. Even very young teens standing in line at Burger King, yakking and fooling around with their peers, yank nervously at jeans sliding excessively low on their hips.

How does one adequately interpret this fussing and fidgeting? The power in self-exposure is volatile and easily wanes. Denuding is preeminently private. Public nudity goes against the grain of females socialized to modesty. Along the life spiral, it is the Toddler—not yet vulnerable to bodily shame—that is unabashedly exhibitionistic. A grownup woman always must choose which exposure of what bodily part will trigger shame. According to Henry Elkin (1966, pp. 168-169), women who enjoy exhibiting themselves hearken back to the healthy two-year old stage. Apropos the epiphany style, the area around the belly is still so preeminently private and vulnerable that very few women become accustomed to exposing it.

Still, in what does the privacy of the privacy consist? What twigs this vulnerability? Is it not because of what the belly, especially "pierced," concretely symbolizes? The depression in the middle of the abdomen marks the point of former attachment of the umbilical cord. The navel naturally alludes to the invisible womb and uterus. Look at the former yolk stalk. It is gone . . . but not forgotten. The button inside the indented tummy is a visible reminder. The algebra of this body-disclosing style also evokes the **unseen** womanly core. The configuration of revealing garments draws the gaze from the female's bare midriff in both directions: north toward the Peaks and south towards the Valley. The total attire makes theme the sensual-sexual **roundness** of breast, nipple and pearl. Consciously or pre-reflectively, it also forges an associative link between the *little hole* at the naval and *the* hole at the *inverted pyramid.*

This bare bellybutton look is not innocent or virginal, and the attitude accompanying it not coy. The mode poses an explicitly genital challenge: "This flat stomach I will flaunt; this bejeweled belly will capture your attention. What you cannot see will draw your eyes. You will want to see it. But it is not for the showing."

Nowadays, women readily initiate even demand sexual performance. All other things being equal, pregnancy is optional. Things never are equal; hence the Pill and the morning after pill. Pregnancy is optional because abortion is an option, either legal or procurable. Has feminine genital power finally been unleashed upon the western world?

Displaying the little hole in the belly button does *not* always signify the consciously deliberate intent to conjure up the genital zone. In living situations, a woman might dress to provoke what might be on a man's mind. But they do not always. As indicated above, most women wear the attire because they think it flatters them. However, the vast majority simply wears whatever clothing is in style. Even though the epiphany mode became passé in the post-election year, still many will continue to wear it for the exact same reason. Besides, less affluent ones cannot afford to buy in one fell swoop a complete new wardrobe just because fashion designers have made a switch.

Selecting clothes during late modernity had become a touchy-thorny problem. How does a woman denude enough to be interesting and desirable without exposing too much to be tagged "sleazy" or "slutty"? How balance dressing fashionably with expressing individuality? Whether or not a particular female dons the garments to strategize seduction deliberately, the epiphany style itself dares to show the *weakest* spot of the woman and to highlight it precisely as her *strongest* place. Thus, an apparent paradox challenges the male. Femininity is flagrantly "in his face" and simultaneously vulnerable. It is far-fetched, is it not, to construe the female belly, even adorned with metal and jewels, as an instrument of power?

This epiphany mode provokes critical questions. Do marginally talented, half-dressed females, darlings of the media, demonstrate feminine power? Does an immensely talented G-string Diva enhance the status of women by blending her multi-octave voice with sensual swagger and exposed skin? Negative answers resound. Filling the coffers of moneymakers drives fashion, not the enhancement of women. A woman bedecked in visible underwear does not exercise optimal control over her body. The look preys upon her bodily insecurities and striving for perfection. It also exposes the alienating price tag many starlets pay to make the front page or get on TV. Slang says they must show the "boys" some "T & A" (tit and ass). The ultra-thin physique demanded by the visible G-string syndrome, natural for fourteen-year-old girls or a pre-pregnant body, sets the female at odds with her biological clock. The strong link between the epiphany look and fad diets, excessive exercise, and surgical weight loss demeans every ripe, mature woman. It symbolizes our *anorexic-bulimic culture*. Fashion is a weapon of the Patriarchy. Shannon Rupp (2004, 2-3) writes:

> Butt-baring jeans rob women of power. Low-rise garments, which make bending and moving difficult, merely perpetuate the oppressive philosophy that women must "suffer" to be beautiful . . . Brainwashing women into accepting the desirability of pain has led to the acceptance of indiscriminate "violence and sexual harassment."

Secondly, she associates the "ass-flash" with the *trailer park lifestyle*. The "low-slung trouser trend" puts woman in her place. Donning it might say, "Sure, women can wear the pants, but only as a symbol of their low status," and she adds with a touch of irony, "Just how much *authority* can any woman claim when she is preoccupied with yanking up her trousers?" (Rupp, 2004, 3). Since no body part is inevitably sexy no matter how bare, a woman does not 'come off' as poised or sensuous while hoisting up her hip huggers or fidgeting with her cropped-top. Rupp insists: "While she may think she's celebrating . . . liberation, it's more likely that . . . the world sees her . . . as an object of lust, contempt, or even ridicule . . . this new moon rising isn't about freedom at all . . . it's just another sign that the sun is setting on woman's power" (Rupp, 2004, 3). The next chapter on beauty and health fleshes out this critique.

Historical Survey of Fashion in Modernity

The waxing and waning of the epiphany mode exemplifies the hypocritical adornment of the female torso throughout modernity. Feminist ideas proliferated at dawning of the twentieth century. The roaring twenties Jazz Age radicalized fashion. By baring the arms and legs, the "flapper" dress shifted demure to risqué. However, the "flapper" is *baggy*, a dress donned to prevent the appearance of promiscuity. After the Great Depression and in between the Great Wars, modest attire quickly returned. Showing cleavage was obscene. Fashion in the '30s shrouded the flesh.

In the 1940s, the garment industry introduces bra *sizes*. For two decades, large **breasts** set the erotic-beauty standard. "Sweater girl glamour" raged. Curvy, busty starlets such as Lana Turner, Jayne Russell, Britt Elkind, Jayne Mansfield, Elizabeth Taylor, and Marilyn Monroe graced the silver screen with something for a man's eyes. The famous picture of Marilyn's décolletage printed in *The American Heritage. Dictionary of the English Language* exposes more than enough to make a man's mouth water.

John Steinbeck (1947, 5) in *The Wayward Bus* captures the historical "moment" with a simple description of the store-restaurant-garage-service station-bus station at Rebels Corners:

> The walls . . . were well decorated with calendars
> and posters showing bright, improbable girls with
> pumped-breasts and no hips—blondes, brunettes and
> redheads, but always with this bust development, so
> that a visitor of another species might judge from the
> preoccupation of artist and audience that the seat of
> procreation lay in the mammeries.

Why at that particular juncture was the USA culture 'hung up' on breasts in almost fetishistic proportions? To repeat, the breasts hold no absolute privilege as an erogenous zone. Without minimizing the primal lure the breast-nipple bond of the original "nursing couple," one can affirm that *visually* breasts are no more inherently beautiful or sensual than other parts of the female structure. Their aesthetically pleasing curvature grabs the eye. As perceptual objects, breasts are mammary glands poised side by side and divided by a cleavage. Insofar as they display curves, they are no more compellingly beautiful than a woman's big round blue eyes, or the lines and indentation of her neck, or her equally curved and (usually bigger) buttocks or the subtle slope that dips from her hips to her Delta. Within the living architecture of a woman's body, the outline of the "triangle" itself and what pornographic rhetoric calls the "camel's toe" are as powerfully alluring as the double globes. Nor is the Delta of Venus the only rival to the 'boobies'. Stark evidence of subtle beauty compels us to interpret this dominance of breasts at mid-20th century. In his epic novel *Russka*, Edward Rutherfurd (1992, 166) describes Yanka coming to womanhood, aware of "a warm, gentle curve around her hips" that men find "delicious." In Mishima's (1973, 6-7) *Spring Snow*, Princess Kasuga subtly turns her head. Kiyoaki glimpses a corner of her mouth. For the first time the full force of womanly beauty strikes him:

> At that moment, a single wisp of hair slipped over her
> clear white cheek, and out of the fine corner of an eye,
> a smile flashed in a spark of black fire. However, the

pure line of her nose did not move. It was as if nothing had happened. This fleeting angle of the Princess's face—too slight to be called a profile—made Kiyoaki feel as if he had seen a rainbow flicker for a bare instant through a prism of pure crystal.

D. H. Lawrence (1976, 203) also describes erotic captivation by the neck:

He noticed the fine, fair down on her cheek and her upper lip, and her soft white neck, like the throat of a nettle flower . . . Her neck made a beautiful line down to her shoulder . . . her forearms looked bright as newly blanched kernels . . . now he noticed her with new eyes.

Whatever is secretive and repressively covered-up tantalizes. The Victorian era so draped the female body from head to foot that there was not supposed to be a **hole** under all those bustles and layers of garments, which precisely digs the "**hole in existence**" that, according to van den Berg (1961, 131-150) marks the spot of our western patriarchy's persistent psychosocial illness.

Victorian men would quiver and quake at any sliver of flesh showing. In Muslim cultures, a man can go mad at spotting just a slim slit of brown flesh showing though a black garment . . . that covers almost everything. Algerian men brag that they can 'see' the female body and shape under all the material by the way the dress falls.

By mid-modernity, the USA had become 'mommy's world'. Her power showed most graphically on the "boob tube" which, quickly after it was marketed, became and remains the nation's "chewing gum for the eyes"—in Frank Lloyd Wright's apt phrase. The *Donna Reed Show* ran from 1958 until 1965. What is the basic plot of *Donna*? She always saved the day. The same occurred on *Father knows best* which ran from 1954 until 1963. Daddy is a loving, well-meaning blunderer. Jackie Gleason, Dick van Dyke—a litany of sitcoms, as well as the newspaper comic *Dagwood and Blondie*—exhibits the male as a bit of a buffoon or a cuddly teddy bear. The power in the family is *not* with dad. Sure, his "heart is in the right place" and his good job pays the bills. Although he brings home the bacon, mom cooks it. No viewer could mistake the fact that Mamma runs the household, even though she pretends that *he* is still the 'king'. Real power squeezes into her 36-24-36 hourglass figure, cup size D.

Betty Crocker's original cookbook was published 1950. Women followed her recipes, heeding propaganda that the best route to a man's heart went through his mouth to his stomach. Nevertheless, in the matter of maternal nourishment, ambivalence reigned. During the 1950s, breast feeding was out of vogue. Mother bottle-fed her baby. A rubber nipple advertised as "more real than the real thing" replaced the fleshy nipple-in-mouth. Mother nurtured her infant without having her breasts sucked . . . out of shape.

Did some wholesome, half-backed idea of the medical profession authorize such forms of madness? It did not. Breasts had assumed a new valence as objects for viewing. Instead of **actively** functioning as imperfectly shaped swollen nipples-to-be-*sucked*-by-a-hungry-mouth-within-*oral*-space, now they should present **passively** as contrived perfectly shaped objects-for-*sighting*-within-the-*visual*-field.

The '40s and '50s pin-up girl was a wholesome cheerleader type with a clear skinned "paper smile" that flashed through perfect white bright teeth. A mandatory millimeter of cleavage highlighted her ample bosom, but unwritten rules forbade showing any bulge of nipple. **A doll**—also a pejorative term describing woman at the time—symbolizes concretely the change. **Barbie**, first sold on 9 March 1959, was on *its* way to becoming a cultural icon (Rogers, 1999).

Mamma was supposed to resemble Barbie: an **irreal**, beautiful, perfectly shaped, fabricated, plastic doll. Mamma should cook, sew, and darn socks, but in addition exaggerate her femininity by sporting an hourglass figure. In what truly describes a hypocritical predicament, however, social mores forbade her to flaunt her natural sexuality.

Marilyn Monroe took Hollywood by storm starting with her first serious role in 1950. Within the next eight years, she made twenty-four films. Like Barbie, Marilyn parodies femininity. The words put into her mouth, "Diamonds are a girl's best friend," announce the same leisure, consumption, and financial dependency that Barbie embodies. Marilyn's persona is a Sex-Goddess poured into costumes such to make ordinary movements impossible. Her image, nevertheless, radiates a wild natural child needing care. Men, who elsewise represent vastly different orientations toward existence, answered her "call." Marilyn's innocent disclaimer of the very eroticism she flaunted smote Arthur Miller, Joe DiMaggio, and John F. Kennedy.

The run-of-the-mill "good enough mother," who had to perform ordinary everyday movements with competence, rejected both the *doll* and the *Doll*. She spurned, too, their impractical clothes that looked not "put on" but "poured into." Until today, the expanded use of Barbie dolls in roles as various classical "princesses" continues to etch images of feminine beauty the "average" living woman cannot approximate.

Historically and politically, the Great War frames the backdrop for this preoccupation with breasts. Nobody knows the ultimate historical judgment about the NATO-USA-British led invasion and occupation of Iraq and the botched ten year military operations in Afghanistan. Both World War I and II, however, were complex failures. Despite achieving *finite* outcomes, the "war to end all wars" resulted in the Iron Curtain, the Berlin Wall, the Cold War . . . and generated coils of revenge that still show no sign of straightening or shrinking. Both wars did succeed in dragging women into the workplace. They succeeded, too, in exposing masculine thinking as pretentiously foolish, and in unmasking the conceptual support of the patriarchy as abstract rationalistic gobbledygook. Witness the perverse ovens and Zylon-B showers of the Holocaust; observe the Mushroom Cloud and Black Rain over Hiroshima and Nagasaki. Truth glares: the life-blood of tenderness and passionate does not quicken western "totalizing" thinking which, contrariwise, comes equipped with built-in lethal imperative for **racism** and **war** (Levinas 1961/1969).

After both wars, the USA built monuments and re-named streets to honor those who died to "save" their country. The nation praised, decorated, and treated as heroes the men in uniform who returned from the European, North African, and Asian theatres. These troopers returned to a permanently altered social world; they themselves came back *stained* by the horrors they had witnessed and psychically endured. Combat had physically maimed or *marked* many; most had killed their fellow humans. Although the culture heaped praise upon the General with two stars as well as upon the Private First Class with simple patches, does not each awarding of the Purple Heart betoken both pride and sorrow?

What do these badges and monuments signify? Craving optimism, the USA hoped the bloodbath had engendered a better world. Honoring warriors both living and dead was preeminently sincere, not lip service. However, daily life did not support official rhetoric. The All-American boy came back home a "Joe Palooka."

When the "boys" sailed from this shore after Pearl Harbor seduced the USA into the fracas, they were budding men, creatures of might and figures to be reckoned with. Like all males in the patriarchy, with unquestioned authority they were lords of all they surveyed. At least they were masters of "their" women. While overseas, however, not a few soldiers sadly received a "Dear John" letter. Psychologists have identified the phenomenon as *anticipatory grief*. A woman, waiting in agony for her man to return from the battleground, grieves his death spontaneously, prematurely, and unto closure. Either while in a foxhole somewhere in France, or upon returning stateside, a soldier learns that his love-bond to wife, fiancée, or girlfriend had dissolved. Once back home, these warriors assume the role of toy soldiers, GI Joe for Barbie dolls to play with. Frolicking popular lyrics asked a playful question "How are you gonna keep them down on the farm, after they've seen Par-ee?" The matter, however, was deadly serious. The war had reversed the social order. The hands of the clock would never turn back. Women wearing trousers held entrenched places in the workforce.

By the 1950's, almost all teachers at the primary levels—and by far most at the secondary levels—were females. According to cultural anthropologist and Freudian-Jungian psychoanalyst, Henry Elkin (1966, 178), this predicament constitutes a historical anomaly since never before had the education of the human mind and the spiritual upbringing of the *male* been entrusted into the hands of women.

The balance of power shifted. The patriarchy seemingly wiggled in death-throes. Men admired, feared, revered, and stared at a woman's "upfront" prominence. Her breasts, the source of ever-flowing nourishment, constituted her power. They had better be big! Moreover, if you have them, flaunt 'em. The culture flaunted them to the max: with blouses that dipped and swooped, with wired bras that pushed them up and forced them out. If you were not well endowed, "falsies" were on sale. You could purchase both the wire and the foam at the "foundations" department at Sears. Since corporate greed perpetuates itself, the fashion and entertainment industries catered to this new reality, co-shaped it, and milked it for all it was worth.

Academia followed suit. By mid-modernity, the university had begun mushrooming into 'the big' business that it is today—a job-training center and degree-factory taking clues from pop culture. Instead of trailblazing, as would befit a citadel for learning, it still follows the mainstream. Back then, the mania for beautiful boobies shows up in adolescent psychology textbooks that depict the development of the breast from its first budding until its maturity. Since system-sanctioned textbooks typically provide "scholarly" support for the mores of the established order, not surprisingly psychologists at mid-century depict the female as "shaped" like Marilyn and Barbie. Psychology students memorize that the final growth of the breast occurs at the average age of sixteen years, at which point the breasts appear *elevated and conical in shape*. Is not that statement existentially and scientifically laughably absurd? Trumpeting *objectivity,* psychologists peddle *as if* scientific fact a male fantasy and the social ideal of the era: sweater girl glamour.

Meanwhile, on the ground mature breasts come in all sizes, shapes, and elevations. In the world of ordinary life, fashion changes. Women begin to burn their bras. Under their colorful tie-dyed shirts, they go bra-less. By the time of the two most well-known events of the late '60's, women were baring it all. The rock opera *Hair* opens on Broadway 29 May 1968; four hundred thousand people attend the open-air festival at Woodstock on 15-17August 1969. It is freedom, independence, and defiance. It is the Age of Aquarius. It might have been the last societal attempt at communal love, harmony between and among racial groups . . . and peace. Hopefully, Occupy Wall Street will usher in a more successful and permanent attempt.

> Unbinding breasts and exposing nipples inherently express radical *revolutionary power:* Unbound breasts show their fluid and changing shape; they do not remain firm and stable objects that phallocentric fetishism desires. Unbound breasts make a mockery of the ideal of a 'perfect' breast . . . . without a bra, nipples show. Nipples are no-no's because they show the breasts to be active and independent zones of sensitivity and eroticism" (Weitz, 1998, 129).

Coupling bare breasts and showcasing a revolutionary vision threatened Uncle Sam, a Puritan at root with a violent underbelly. The '60s Vision rejects materialism, defies authority, protests against the Vietnam War, support civil rights movements, dresses unconventionally, experiments with sex and recreational drugs . . . and preaches that love is the mainspring of Life.

Every socio-political movement spawns excesses. To some citizens the '60s is synonymous with the dirty word "hippie," invoked to stigmatize counterculture citizens. Hippie connotes free love and free sex, "free" taken to mean irresponsible, careless sex performed with too little soap and too few showers . . . and inter-racial sex to boot! Narrow-minded reactionaries will always identify the '60s, not by the Peace sign, but by naked breasts and protruding nipples. Puritan-violent-racist Americans found the movement far too much to the left and the tied-dyed shirts more than a little too 'pink.' All the righteous rightwing enjoyed about the '60s, besides the wonderful music were the . . . naked views.

Other doers and thinkers, however, will remember the '60s as a time when gentle souls tried to "make love not war" and were horribly disillusioned. Power dressed them in 'proper' attire and cut the very hair off their heads.

The conservative backlash against radical revolutionary excesses creates excesses. *Hair* opens for a short run at the Shakespeare Public Theatre on 17 October 1967 (eventually opening on Broadway at the Biltmore Theatre on 29 April 1968). It closes on 1 July 1972 after 1,742 performances. Initially, this controversial "American Tribal-Love Rock Opera" evokes extreme public contempt insofar as it features nudity, obscenity, and desecration of the American flag. It prompts two prominent law cases. In Chattanooga, the Supreme Court of Tennessee (1975) describes it as "lewd and lascivious" and anti-American. The Supreme Court of Massachusetts, held in Boston (1970) specifies that the staging the production could take place on condition that clothing *be worn to a reasonable extent* at all times by each cast member, and mandatory elimination of the simulation of sexual intercourse or deviation.

This is the era of Richard Millhouse Nixon, elected President in 1968. Since we have not yet received permission to listen to all the tapes he recorded, we still are not 100% certain if his White House was decayed or sporting a new coat of paint. Even without complete evidence, we witnessed on all the major networks his paranoid ways inflicting *reactionary violence*. Before the eyes of the Nation, his right-winged force beat to a pulp "protestors." Such governmental terror erupts unexpectedly at Kent State

University in Ohio. It flares, too, in a very predictable spot during the Democratic National Convention in Chicago.

The weave of eroticism and power has never been more very visible before or afterwards. On all social fronts, a backlash was imminent. The right-winged establishment set about curtailing not only freedom, but also public nudity. Arguably, it co-operates in the killing of Martin Luther, Robert and John F. Kennedy. A radical switch in fashion-themes is inevitable.

Twiggy wiggles to center stage in the popular imagination, the first mass-merchandized model. Born Lesley Hornby, her career spanned 1966-1969. At the time, at age seventeen years she is the most famous model on the planet, appearing on the cover of *Vogue* magazine four times. Doe-eyed, with 31-22-32 measurements and carrying barely ninety pounds on her 5'6" frame, her figure perfectly displaces the lush soft round sensual-sexual shapes of the Age of Aquarius. Her physique is "the frail torso of a teenage choirboy . . . four straight limbs in search of a body" (Twiggy 2005). The famous London photographer, Richard Avedon, describes hers the "face of 1966," and claims she "embodied the boldness and the innocence of her era" and that her movements in front lights "conveyed the *air of her age* . . . and brought her generation in front of the camera" (Twiggy, 2005).Wearing a lime-green mini skirt and green tights, Twiggy ushers in the "ultra-thinning of women" as the criterion of a beautiful body.

Mini-skirts are 'in'. By the mid-late 1960's and early 1970s, women had worn the pants long enough. Now, it was time to take them off and to show what was under them. Well not exactly! In the style of the mini-skirt, fashion reveals lovely *legs* as the symbolic substitute for what women at the end of Victorian times had ardently desired, and what modern women claimed as theirs: the *phallus,* the arch-symbol of equality.

The new sensual montage consisted of long, lean and shapely legs, accented by high-heeled platform shoes to accent the calf and to display pantyhose. Eventually, the commercial would blare: "Legs! You've got legs!" Now men feast their eyes on the limb from ankle to the upper thigh, just a few tantalizing inches shy of the Delta. The male gawk might strain to see the panties that covered the bush, but the design of the mini skirt does not expose underwear. The configuration does make easy, nonetheless, a quick short move that would accidentally flash them. At her own discretion, any woman could.

Legs have a loveliness of their own, too. Who would doubt it? However, they are no more sexy or sensuous than arms or the small of the back. Why did legs become lust objects at this point in history? Again, leaning upon Henry Elkin (1966), legs represent the *Phallic Mother*. Who is she? She is the 'hard' mother; the competitive, power-oriented, rule-driven, 'bossy' mother; the woman with a "kick"; a throwback to the Amazons of the original Matriarchy.

Women, poised to beat men at their own game, now stride for power differently. Identity is no longer totally rooted in and limited to roles of wife and / or mother. The soft, drug-mellowed love of the Age of Aquarius had failed. Offering the bared breast and tender nipple had not secured a more humane society. Now, women would strut on legs. "These booths are made for walking," sings Nancy Sinatra, conveying two messages. Strong legs in boots would give the woman a sense of power. If she prefers, she could now walk away from the man. Total dependency was ancient history. The equality and freedom in the wind also creep into legislation. A legal battle would rage in 1976 over the Equal Rights Amendment. The male is about to become "just dessert."

During this last quarter of the 20th century, the frameworks also dramatically changes in intellectual discourse and social existence. In cyberspace and in the Global Village, conflicting ideologies jostle briskly as modernity reluctantly yields to postmodernity. The "Yuppie" elbows out the "Hippie," thus highlighting the *class character* of embodiment and fashion. Under the sway of the Yuppie, liberal and communal ideals decay into greed, desire for individualistic success, and concerns about security, achievement, glamour, and self-aggrandizement. As we still reel economically in 20011 as a result of the financial fallout of 2008, only the 1% that the Occupy Wall Street makes theme does not suffer from the climate of greed.

Concerning fashion, the epiphany of flesh at the millennium erupts against the backdrop of cyberbodies. The urban landscape, massaged by a steady diet of mass media images, transmutes into a consumer society of burgeoning affluent middle-class professionals and managers. The self transforms into a performer, parading hysterically within a culture of performances. The spectacles of the "technological bazaar" keep switching, kaleidoscopically; the body keeps altering under the power of dieting, fitness-training, body building, and tanning, health farms and fat farms, prescription pills, and the surgeon's knife . . . body modifications and prosthetics. Simulation and hyperrealization eclipse traditional "reality." Social interaction mediated by technology holds sway. The lines between illusion or virtual reality and reality blur. Mass-media image-seduction converges with yuppiefied self-performances, reshaping the body, recasting sexuality, and feeding the fashion industry. In the next chapter, we will discuss the unhealthy effect this has on women.

Popular trends reveal the spirit of the times with more transparency than volumes of academic accounts. In them we glimpse the mores and ruling ideas that actually move and shake the social scene. The artifacts of popular culture mirror their historical circumstances and lay bare the hidden political-economic conditions in which they emerge. In 1976, the portrayal of women on television sandwiches the raging political debate about Equal Rights. While watching *Wonder Woman, Charlie's Angels* and *The Bionic Woman*, we also witness vividly the influence of visual culture and electronic mediation, the way society constructs the female body, and how powerful vested interests sabotage the feminist's project of equality and liberation.

The consumer-visual culture of the late 1970s exhibits a flexible, plasticized, and technologically modified body. The body was a lifestyle accessory to be stylized, sculpted, and shaped. The grassroots movements of the 1960s and ideological feminism had failed to dismantle patriarchal edifices. White, middle-class males with power and money resent the emerging group of single, working women. The entertainment industry finally figures out ways to take advantage of the Women's Liberation trend and simultaneously to contain it. Western culture's ingrained metaphysical prejudices persist. Its negativity towards embodiment and its dread of fragility and tenderness assumes different shapes, but it also deepens.

Wonder Woman, a super-hero created as a cartoon character in 1941, comes to life on the screen on 1 December 1976 in the guise of "glamorous and shapely" Lynda Carter. Miss America in 1973 representing Arizona, Lynda, stands 5'9" and according to *Celebrity Sleuth* magazine measures in her costume a very non-Twiggy like 37 1/2C-25-35. Wonder Woman is Princess Diana, a natural beauty who descends from the ancient Greek Amazons. Her powerful tools are classical masculine weapons: a golden lasso, metal bracelet, metal crown, and a fantastically surreal airplane. Unlike the bra-less, bare-breasted, counter-culture woman of the 1960's, she defends the Established Order with staunch, fearless commitment. Executing her mandatory twirls during each episode, she reveals pronounced curves, an ample bosom, and strong beautiful legs. However, her sexual flesh is so background that paradoxically it is actually foreground. The viewer can't miss it, but it has no role in the plots. Wonder Woman fits comfortably within the patriarchy.

Charlie's Angels likewise represent culturally sanctioned and supervised feminine independence. The *Angels* debuts 22 September 1976 and runs until 1981, featuring Farrah Fawcett, Kate Jackson, and Jaclyn Smith. Farrah plays the role of a sexy vivacious phallic heroine. Chadwick Roberts (2003, 86) describes in detail her red swimsuit poster, "the bestselling pin-up of all-time" that features her long legs and "decidedly exposed inner thigh . . . but gone are the ample hips and breasts." Like Wonder Woman, "Farrah's poster mediates the fear and unease that resulted from the sexual revolution of the '60s . . . and reinstates a clean wholesomeness into sexual visible culture . . . it is liberated without being dangerously exposed . . . a contrived 'natural' look [that] embodies "enlightened conformity" (Roberts, 2003, 87). Aaron Spelling, executive producer for *Charlie's Angles*, brags that the Angels' sex appeal and appearance matter most: "On this show we're more concerned with hairdos and gowns than the twists and turns of the plots . . . anyone who thinks these girls are really private detectives is nuts" (O'Hallaren 1976, 26).

Vignette of a Cyborg: The Bionic <?>

Let us delve more deeply into one other piece of popular culture. The first female cyber-body on prime time television is Jamie Sommers. This series clearly mirror its historical circumstances, anticipates our cyber-world, and lays bare the hidden political-economic conditions of its time.

The lovely Lindsay Wagner plays *The Bionic Woman*, premiering in January 1976 as an immediate hit and running for three seasons. Jaime has two bionic legs, a bionic right arm and a bionic ear that allows her to hear a whisper a mile away. Her 'superhuman' powers include the ability to run 60 mph, bend steel with her bare hands, jump to the roof of a 12 story building and catch villains endangering the national security of the USA.

The Bionic Woman ushers into popular culture a new bodily dualism. Weekly on the TV screen, the blurred boundaries between biological, natural human body and the artificial technical hybrid confront the average citizen. Jamie also harbingers technological body modifications and our current obsession with "extreme" make-over procedures and the raging theological-political debate over stem cell research.

Jamie is a traditional female masquerading as a 'new' breed of the '70s woman. Male supremacy blitzes the series. Oscar, who gave Jamie life after her near fatal accident, controls her from pillar to post. Without even consulting her, he procures her a salvage worker position. At the work site, Jamie dresses in overalls and boots like one of the 'boys' and functions in step with them. However, she wears pigtails, twirls her hair, lowers her eyes, plays with a kitten, and in certain situations resorts to a young girl's tone of voice. Regularly, she complies, pacifies, and goes girlish in order to gain information or accomplish her aims. The entire series, in fact, pivots around the father-daughter relationship. For instance, in obviously non-sexual, non-sensuous ways, Jamie hugs and kisses her coworkers—comportment they never ape. So sexism, male ignorance and patriarchal prejudices run rampant throughout the episodes. The 1960s' revolutions had publicly and furiously assaulted the patriarchy. The *Bionic Woman* embraces phallocentrism and cradles male dominance.

This vignette of Jamie unmasks political motives. Powerful vested interests, 'Masculinist dreams of body transcendence and ... attempts at body repression', restructure and re-assemble a new hybrid female body .... according to cultural and ... ideological standards of physical appearance (Balsamo, 1996, 233; 226). Thus, the burgeoning 1970s cyborgian technology covers the bare breasts of the Age of Aquarius, curtails the liberated sexuality of Woodstock, and sabotages the feminist's project of equality and liberation.

Since this popular program successfully realizes the desire to return to bodily neutrality and be rid of the culturally marked body, it provides a metaphor for today's traffic along the information highway. Visual technological images serve as regressive and reactionary weapons of power and social control (Foucault, 1975/1979). In spite possessing incredible powers, patriarchal oedipal dynamics trap the Bionic Woman.

Our tale loops full circle. If the naked body is a revolutionary signifier, the draped flesh "reveals" counter-revolutionary aims. Mid-2005 marks the historical "moment" of **neo-conservatism.** More than any other time in history, *success and security* obsess USA citizens. They would prefer to protect their personal patch of ground and to **cover** their flanks. This right-winged pattern pertains to the themes of this essay because its conceptual journey leads to a clear decisive idea: *fashion reveals the fatal flaw in western thinking, an unremitting contempt for the flesh-cum-financial greed.* Whether making choices for clothing, or opting to make war, a nerve of *nihilism, that is a life-denying, denigrating ideology* coils around western man's heart and head.

Greed and contempt glare in the hypocrisy that underpins our anorexic-bulimic culture. By the 1990s, eating disorders had gobbled up five million women in America. It's absurd, is it not, that a privileged, affluent, obese American culture is starving itself? Bulimia, anorexia nervosa, and obesity are *culture chaos disorders*, a controlling way of responding to cultural transitions. Keel and Klump (2003) find a low prevalence of anorexia and no bulimia outside western societies, and they document the absence of any cogently compelling evidence of a biological-medical explanation for the disorders. If you would seek financial support for a research project to study them *in the Sudan,* you would elicit scorn. In Sudan, there exists the real eating disorder. *The basic eating disorder is starvation from a lack of food, not the refusal to eat for reasons of "body image."* Basic eating disorders root in the horrendous gap between the "stuffed and the starved," slide in the crack of the shameful fact that dire poverty and greedy wealth co-exist in the western world. Thus, clinical diagnoses of bulimia and anorexia nervosa above all disguise the painful and alienating sides of our cultural dis-ease: the profit-motive. Equally, they serve as metaphors of Western civilization's persistent illness: refusal to cherish human embodiment.

The *human* being and the *rat*, demonstrates Fred Wertz (1986), are the only creatures on the planet that destroy their own kind for pleasure and profit. Food and drugs are domains where show the destructive consequences of capitalism's insatiable drive to sell products. G. Edward. Griffin (2003, 211) documents the "conspiracy" whereby the marriage between political opportunists and the international cartels of the oil and pharmacy plan and execute global wars, reaping gigantic profits with investment in the arts of *wounding* and *healing.* In a statement pertinent to our contemporary geopolitical predicament, Griffin (2003, 212) says it's easy to pull the wool over the eyes of a naive and ignorantly trusting public: "When one wishes to wage war or regain his health, he seldom questions the price."

Slimness-cum-clothing as a feminine ideal co-constitutes the pressing problem of eating disorders. Commercials promoting gluttony bombard the American public; yet our cultural icons are those who so resist the lure that they . . . starve themselves. While health providers worry that an epidemic of bulimia-anorexia nervosa rages largely *not diagnosed*, the main mission of the System is to shrink obesity. This is especially because, I repeat, an increasing number of American children are "living extra-large." Instead of focusing squarely on the horrific infant-baby-child diets the food industry packages which is the root of childhood obesity, the System broadcasts that the problem can begin at *any* age. Lo and behold, "fortunately" commerce has formulated a solution: "lean" food for kids. The buck passes and the blubber goes on.

Where else than in a children's storybook is hypocrisy most pernicious? Barbie again! Barbie and friends are having a sleepover party, a fingernail party to be exact. While Barbie warms up mini pizzas, the "girls" discuss possible toppings, such as pepperoni. "Yuck," says Midge, *grabbing a cookie and dipping it in whipped cream.* Teresa reprimands her for eating dessert first. "That's okay," giggles Barbie, "as long as she saves room for dinner!" (Pompa, 1999, 5).

CHAPTER SEVENTEEN

Under Siege: A Woman's Beauty and Health[6]

Each woman is beautiful in her own particular way. But in showing no democratic inclinations, Nature, God, the Buddha, Yahweh, and Allah distribute beauty unevenly. It is preposterous to imagine it otherwise. A woman is not reducible to a sophisticated computer or a highly evolved mammal. She is an earthling whose beauty is subject to the contingencies of frail flesh. Her beauty is fragile.

Over the millennia, consequently, women have augmented their appearance by highlighting their best traits and hiding real or imagined flaws. They have adorned themselves with paraphernalia such as body paint, rings, bones, beads, jewels, girdles, garters, corsets, and falsies; and with lipstick, rouge, mascara, eye shadow, and false eyelashes. They have clipped, curled, braided, styled, and colored their hair. They have availed themselves of their culture's technologies to makeover their facial features and body shape. Beauty is always interlaced with sexuality, self, seduction, vanity, exhibitionism, attracting a mate, creating family, health, and luxury. It is the way of the world. Who would gainsay it?

The weave of a woman's health and beauty is the theme of this chapter. Its specific focus is the menace to a woman's entire existence that the marriage of late capitalism and the western

---

6   Under Siege: A woman's beauty and health." Presented to Woman's Health: Science, Technology, and Society. St. Francis College, Brooklyn, N.Y. 2 April, 2011.

patriarchy generates. A plethora of commercial enterprises take advantage of the idiosyncratic appearance and uneven distribution of beauty to exploit it to the harm of a woman's health. This chapter depicts the siege under which a conglomerate of industries has put a woman's entire existence: her beauty, health, body, sexuality, sense of self, and even her opportunities for employment. Medical aesthetics, pharmacy, cosmetics, fashion, bodily modification, diet, hair, the spa, and so forth menace women's beauty and heath. These commercial entities huddle under the banner of health where they collectively reduce beauty to a product, reap massive financial profit by peddling lies that disregard the woman's genuine health and in the process defile her beauty. Secondly, the chapter exposes the unconscionable support that mainstream medico-social-anthropological scholarship gives to this siege.

Beauty in the Everyday Lifeworld

I begin with my story that puts into context my entire article and, indeed, captures its essence.

> In the heart of Manhattan sits the Museum of Modern Art (MoMA).Yesterday, two art critics visited it to write a review of recent acquisitions. I watched them traipse with pad and pen discussing various works and debating art theory. They agreed on **nothing**. One painting in particular fired their wrath. The shorter of the two theoretical experts raised his voice and the tall one shook his fist. Before violence could erupt a women strolled in front of the two men, caught their eyes, spoke something seemingly insightful, and then slowly sashayed away. One critic's eyes popped out; the other's jaw dropped. Both turned their heads and uttered, simultaneously, "W-W-WOW . . . G-r-r-r-r."

This narrative depicts the ever widening gap between action in everyday life and scientific accounts based upon abstract, arbitrary ideology. The common folk know well what eludes the 'experts'. I gather phenomenological data by asking participant-subjects in various groups to respond to: "When you see woman and say that she is beautiful (or a man and call him handsome) please describe to what in the individual are you responding?"; "Whenever you think you look your most beautiful or handsome describe what gives you that confidence." The results of my analysis, using Amedeo Giorgi's (2009) method, require a separate article. In a nutshell, the data reveal that ordinary people in everyday situations spontaneously recognize beauty, understand that it differs across cultures, history, and the life spiral, and appreciate it as a unique emergence between two individuals. It does not befuddle the common people that the beauty of a young lass coming into her womanhood differs from that of a woman in the prime of her life, nor perplex them that Cleopatra's beauty does not equate with Elizabeth Taylor's when the late actress was in her prime; nor do they fear that beauty means nothing definite since the African man hankers after big butts whereas dudes in Hollyweid like their women long and lean.

Academic researchers reverse the situation. They cannot agree upon a single operational definition of beauty. They find it culturally relative, differing across continents, changeable over history, and variable within pockets of contemporary time. Consequently, researchers tag beauty an "elusive concept" and flounder when they try to study it (Edmonds & van den Geest, 2009, 5). The literature on the topic, therefore, is rationally chaotic and empty.

It is the same with health. Researchers bemoan its ambiguity. They find it as difficult to pinpoint as theologians trying to define God with a negative definition. By their own admission these disciplines stumble in the attempt to understand it. The best idea they venture is that health is more than the "absence of illness" (Edmonds and van den Geest, 2009, 8). But they have nothing to say about the 'more,' and lack any sense of the affirmative power which constitutes the essence of health. Scholarly equivocation about these two important phenomena—as we shall see below—leads to bankrupt findings.

What underwrites this scholarly ineptitude? Philosophical rationalism, dualism, and positivism hold sway over mainstream scientific disciplines. Mainstream researchers, rooted in 19th century natural science, subscribe to the quantitative imperative. Their normative processes of generating objective information handicap efforts to understand matters relevant to the human heart and pertinent to the networks of relationships between individuals and among peoples. Instead of genuinely bringing truth to light about these important realities, medico-social scientists shelter the profit motive, foster greed, and cogenerate destructive action and outcomes.

Needed to curtail such arbitrary, rationalistic, pseudo-objective blindness is a shift in conceptual paradigm and a change of heart—a *metanoia*. My human scientific study stands upon the platform of existential phenomenological psychology. It adopts the Life-world as its privileged laboratory for researching day-to-day flesh and blood experience. In today's common parlance, I stay close to the ground and within the fluid temporal flow of each day to study precious lived experiences and personal meanings.

An Unholy Marriage

In the nuptial bed which Late Capitalism and the Patriarchy share, a slew of commercial enterprises congregate: cosmetics, fashion, aesthetic medicine, the pharmaceutical industry, marketing and advertising, mass media, entertainment, bodily modification programs, fitness centers, health and beauty spas, hair salons, and diet industries. Within this loose alliance Power and Money rules. Beauty serves the profit motive.

These capitalistic enterprises generate their profit by pedaling propaganda and fabricating counterfeit images of beauty. Make no bones about it. Nobody looks like *Playboy's* Miss January. The model's contrived beautiful face and body existed radiantly only in the eye blink it took to take the photo. And only touching her nipples with ice cubes the instant before the shutter snapped enlarged them such to pop a man's eyes out.

Confabulation! Chernin (1991), while making theme the "tyranny of slenderness," demonstrates the connection between the contrived value of being slim and the epidemics of bulimia and anorexia nervosa: Beauty = thinness. Kaw (1993) further unmasks the racism that laces the politics of attractiveness: Beauty = white skin.

The confabulated images of beauty serve another purpose: indoctrination. *No woman is beautiful enough. Every woman must improve her looks.* Women sop up the demand as an existential imperative. The various business concerns, of course, tender expensive treatments to come to her rescue. There are almost as many remedies for enhancing appearance and eradicating flaws as there are . . . snowflakes in Scandinavia.

Who—and the question burns—is the woman procuring the treatments, wearing the clothes in vogue, applying cosmetics, taking injections of Botox, swallowing diet pills, getting a boob or butt job, or . . . having her colon accidently punctured with a liposuction needle? She is *nobody*. She is algebraic. Beauty matters to business and industry only insofar as it is marketable. Fashion, pharmacy, and aesthetic surgery could care less about a woman as a unique, concrete, and singular person. Clothing and cosmetics make money. Moneymakers do not value the natural appearance of a woman, or quibble about standards of beauty, or quarrel about aesthetic ideals. They count coins. Pragmatic thinking holds sway.

The philosophical idea of pragmatism is simple: that which works is true = what sells is beautiful. Medical aesthetics, pharmacy, advertising, fashion, and the media, I repeat, manufacture beauty as a trick to rake in the dough. If Twiggy makes big bucks, then hers was the "face of the age"; if Miss Piggy sells seats at the cinema and successfully pedals the movie's related paraphernalia, whatever 'she' is, she is lovely (Alapack, 2009). If Lady Gaga is today's princess of pop and the eleventh most powerful woman in the world in 2011 (as *Forbes* magazine professes), then her anticipated nude photo shoot for Playboy will sell CDs and the clothing-cum-accoutrements of the Gothic look—to the ill health of our young girls.

Is this ordinary exercise in democratic capitalism harmless? Should we begrudge the profiteers and medical merchants for earning their daily bread by taking advantage of Life's uneven distribution of beauty? None of us are innocent enough, are we, to balance the scales of greed and vanity with wisdom and integrity? But the stakes are higher than ethical purity. Because why?

Randomly, the so-called treatments and remedies for ugliness, or fat tummies, or small breasts, or big noses, or flat butts boomerang. The dubious healing arts severely harm health. It suits to pay attention to the 'friendly fire' that occurs during the exercises in 'preventive diplomacy' and 'preventive war' that the dialectic of beauty and health masks. All of a sudden we might find ourselves facing 'collateral damage'.

Aesthetic Medicine

The phrase "aesthetic medicine" rings with the same false notes, does it not, as other politico-military mendacious phrases coined to blur deception: 'friendly fire', 'extraordinary rendition', 'collateral damage', 'preventive diplomacy', preventive war'? Nobody believes that cosmetic surgery concerns heath. "Cosmetic procedures," Edmond (2009, 31) writes, "can never be justified as health practices." Aesthetic medicine is intrinsically braided with the consumer culture of Late Capitalism. Whatever rhetoric its proponents spout, plastic surgery reduces beauty to a commodity 100% of the time. When you think of silicon, think of greed. Hold in mind that Brazil, with its cheap and abundant services of *plástica* has become a top destination for *medical tourism* (Edmonds, 2009, 23).

In order to do its deeds, the practice of cosmetic surgery must hold in abeyance questions about beauty and health and bracket concerns about surgical risks and possible untoward outcomes. To authorize body contouring and radical physical changes, it leans upon presumed positive values and benign intentions, e.g. that the procedures will increase self-esteem. Simply put, it accepts the questionable premise of cognitive behavioral technology: a perceived positive change in thinking or in behavior will reinforce the change and leads to more positive outcomes.

Cosmetic surgery is never medically necessary either, but is always elective. No one can claim that it improves physical health or saves lives. A woman and her doctor (with or without family consultation or consent) choose breast operations, facelifts, liposuction, genital cosmetic surgery, labiaplasty, post-partum correction, vaginal rejuvenation. Historically, doctors performed cesarean sections to safeguard the welfare of the child or the mother. With alarming frequency women nowadays also elect them for non-clinical reasons—translate as 'aesthetic' reasons . . . translate as reasons of 'vanity'. Justification for sterilization and tubal ligation fall into the same box of . . . warped words . . . Medical tourism and preventative war indeed!

Cosmetic surgery, moreover, does not even guarantee beauty enhancement. 'Monkeying around' with the breasts, tummy, or nose often results in new defects more repulsive than the original flaws. Unattractive scar tissue commonly results. Or the intended correction for flaccid breasts might result in something much worse than mere scars. Imagine opening your eyes on the operating table and seeing your two nipples pointing in opposite directions.

Like any form of surgery, *plástica* carries risks. Post-operative infections occur as do adverse reactions to anesthesia or foreign substances inserted into the body. I personally know an incident more terrible than a surgeon accidently pricking the colon with a liposuction needle. A South African woman, a dear personal friend, died on the operating table when the 'accident' went undetected. The surgeon had punctured her aorta.

Reconstructive surgery

also has its pitfall. Concerning cancer, Karakasidou (2008) identifies a current conspiracy of silence. Reconstructive surgery conceals the breast mutilated by cancer. Physicians and patients proudly render the 'face' of cancer socially normal and aesthetically beautiful. The horrible truth that cancer is a beauty-body destroying disease goes missing. In the ruse of seemingly restoring beauty, surgery denies the *angst* of a terminal illness.

A New View of a Woman's Sexuality

At the manufacture of Sildenafil citrate, sold as Viagra, Leonore Tiefer foresaw what has come to pass: the medicalization of both men and women's sexual problems. For more than a dozen years, she has been unmasking systematically, rigorously, and relentlessly the "disease-mongering trends" in the medical management of women's sexuality (Tiefer, 2011). Put differently, her "New View Campaign" has been trying to halt the siege under which the pharmaceutical industry in cahoots with the medical establishment has put a woman's sexuality. Labiaplasty and vaginal rejuvenation are just two vanity-greed driven procedures. The pharmaceutical industry peddles its drugs allegedly promoting sexual health. Its deceptive advertising masks the existential side-effects that put at risk a woman's physical-psycho-spiritual-sexual health.

Sheltering the Siege

Beauty dazzles us. Money-makers find it ready-at-hand to warp, pursue as a commodity, and milk from it all the shekels they can shake. Should it not be the task of those doers and thinkers, paid by the System as professionals and academics, to call a halt to the siege? Sadly, the opposite is true. Mainstream scholars, wittingly or unwittingly, shelter it. Held hostage by a rationalistic ideology, most scientific researchers flounder because they cannot coin a consensual operational definition or univocal concept of health or beauty, and cannot identify a cross-cultural absolute standard or an objective criterion for beauty and health. Instead, medico-anthropological-social scientists wallow within abstract dualistic dilemmas.

Psychologists in particular hang themselves on the hooks of the decrepit nature-nurture dichotomy: Is beauty the product of biological evolutionary adaptation or socially constructed? All we get is a 50-50 split in the debate and hollow research findings. The failure to comprehend common and significant phenomena ultimately leads to destruction. Our academics and professionals collude with, support, or at least turn a blind eye to practices that compromise the integrity of women. It suits to exemplify.

According to Tiefer (2011), research on woman's sexuality is almost entirely funded by the pharmaceutical industry. It is hopelessly naïve to doubt that this practice of buying scientific evidence is limited to sexology. I witnessed it in spades to my horror when I functioned as clinical-community director of the Seward Life Action Council in the wake of the Exxon Valdez oil catastrophe in 1989 (Alapack, 1991). I learned that the State of Alaska didn't want truth, facts, or even a "clean up"; the politicians preferred a "whitewash" (Alapack, 2010, 230). I also learned the truth of Foucault's (1975/1979) assertion that power dictates knowledge.

Honestly but kindly Tiefer (2000) suggests that researchers have struck a Faustian bargain. But welcome funding and increased professional opportunities come at a price. Serious ethical, political, theoretical, and research questions loom and linger.

While "analyzing the dynamic and sometimes conflicting relationship between beauty and health," the medical anthropologist, Alexander Edmonds (2009, 21) trips very badly on his theoretical paradigm. Although he unmasks the flaws of medical aesthetics, he shelters it with a mind-body split: "Plastic surgery becomes a form of healing that targets not an ugly or aging body but rather a suffering mind . . . . it becomes a medical necessity worthy of public funding" (Edmonds, 2009, 23). Although he recognizes that aesthetic surgery is a parasite already burdening medical systems worldwide, nevertheless he capitulates to the medical money-merchants: "Most patients say that they not only look better after procedures, but they feel better too" (Edmonds, 2009, 22). Diminishing social sigma and minimizing mental dissatisfaction, therefore, authorize surgery as healing. Since he views notions of beauty, health and healing as historically contingent and culturally relative, Edmonds concludes that procedures are medically necessary because they augment self-esteem, make one feel better, and thus promote health and happiness (Edmonds. 2008). The argument is rational and dualistic. It mimics the bankrupt promise of behaviorism: that if we make external, surface changes, then everything else will take care of itself.

Within that conceptual framework, Edmonds feebly condones the Brazilian practice of giving a girl 'coming of age' the "present of a breast job" (2009, 25). [Norwegian mothers give their daughters such a present at the time of their Confirmation]. Edmonds' justification for medical aesthetics is that better looking breasts foster well-being and temporarily boost self-esteem. Suspend belief in that ruse and truth glares: performing plastic surgery on the breasts of a fourteen year old girl is unconscionable. We lack information on the long term medical effects of such a procedure. Preemptive diplomacy again: The girl is pleased! Doctors collect fees; researchers procure grants. Friendly fire . . .

Goths and Emos

Body cutting, anorexia nervosa, and bulimia have reached epidemic proportion. The complexity of the problems is mind-boggling. We have no simple explanation for either. But these dis-eases express one common meaning: they demonstrate *protest.* They are anti-establishment acts. In particular, they express a radical refusal to accept the culturally stereotypic views of beauty. They reject the beauty-trap.

Lina Cristina Casado i Marin (2011) has explored the meanings of bodily self-harm and suicidal thinking by analyzing dialogue and relationship of youth in Online virtual communities. One striking finding is that young girls inflict self-harm in quest of a new view of beauty. Scars to Goths and Emos are beautiful. Dark Rose says, "I am as beautiful and special as my scars" (Casado, 2011, 79). A painful way, is it not, to escape the beauty-trap? In a chilling reversal, young girls repudiate what academics and professionals condone. It's not supposed to be that way.

Botox: Anti-Wrinkle Anti-Soul

The beauty trap has ensnarled Kerry Campbell. She is "beauty-pageant obsessed" and wants to give her daughter, Britney, the edge to become Miss Teen America (Pearce, 2011). "I'm injecting my eight-year-old with Botox and getting her body waxed so she'll be a superstar" she bragged defiantly on 12 May 2011 to a national audience on *Good Morning America* (Pearce, 2011).

Like other preteens, Britney "loves dancing to Lady GaGa, is fond of fashion, and enjoys putting on make-up" (Pearce, 2011). But she shares her mother's capture: the poison of propaganda converted to indoctrination and internalized. "I check every night for wrinkles," she says, "when I see some I want more injections. They used to hurt, but now I don't cry that much. I also want a boob and nose job soon, so I can be a star."

San Francisco Human Services took custody of Britney. Investigation revealed that Kelly's real name is Sheena Upton. Although she asked for forgiveness, she also claimed that the Botox matter was a hoax, a publicity stunt to help her become a 'reality television' star.

Is truth even more elusive than either beauty or health? Frightening 'real', nonetheless, are the annual 25,000 beauty pageants that parade little girls between the ages of 4-to 8 years-olds. Launched a half century ago, this lucrative pageant industry has mushroomed into a concern raking in a billion dollar per year. Who gives a hoot about "collateral damage?"

Raw Beauty

Beauty is holistic. Arguably, the best word to comprehend it is "physiognomy." Beauty encompasses face, figure, a woman's mien, the way she carries herself, moves, and gestures, the ways she speaks, and her so-called personal, intellectual, moral, and spiritual characteristics. Beauty is a total package. A beautiful woman inspires trust with her elegance and grace, steadfastness and suppleness, pliancy and charm (Alapack, 2007, 182-183).

Physiognomy denotes unity. The Greek words, *physis* means nature and *gnomos* means the knower. Beauty shows itself of self and also appears to someone. There is no absolute beauty. One appears beautiful to another; or one finds someone beautiful. Sometimes it is easy to account for. Sometimes it is mysterious. The common folk see this clearly.

Disfigured Beauty: The Splendor of Dancing

Alfonso Lingis (2011) gives us a portrait of beauty that destroys the illusory Hollyweird version that holds sway nowadays. Sonia, he tells us, is thirty-five years old from the Dominican Republic. Living on welfare, she received a grant to attend a conference in Australia. Breast cancer had already ravaged her full mature woman's body. At the meeting in Sidney on culture studies, she did a performance. Naked, except for a skullcap of white feathers, she danced. "Her left breast was a mound of discolored flesh with no nipple; a thick crooked scar extended across her lower abdomen" (Lingis, 2011, 129). Sonia's butchered flesh gives living proof that without being able to afford expensive private care, botched surgery is all she got. But she could dance. And in dancing, her body undergoes a metamorphosis. Lingis (201, 129-30) writes:

> Sonia danced at a distance from where we stood, but across that distance her nakedness made contact with our bodies. Her fear for mortal flesh infected us; we felt a visceral sense of the vulnerability of our bodies sheathed beneath clothing renewed each day. The shadow of death closed in upon us. At the same time, her nakedness revealed her courage and her determination . . . . . Dance: it's movement that is not going anywhere. This absolute movement, wholly in the present, transfigured her body: in all her nakedness she was wholly beautiful [with] a beauty that enthralled us . . . . and as we glanced at one another, somehow

the beauty of our bodies, young and old, thick or thin, muscled or sagging glowed.

Russian Journal

John Steinbeck and Robert Capa visited Stalingrad in the summer of 1947. They found a city destroyed by Nazi rocket and shell fire. "Underneath the rubble were cellars and holes," Steinbeck (1999, 115) writes, "and in these holes many people lived." He describes a terrifying mockery to the veneer of modern fashion and to the travesty of contemporary women who 'shop until they drop' seeking beauty in make-up, clothing, beauty shops, and in major makeovers, in cosmetic surgery, in breast augmentation or reduction. His word picture is the absolute foil to the quest for artificial beauty through the use of Power and Money. For the duration of his stay in Stalingrad, early every morning he would watch a young girl crawling out of one of these holes.

> She had long legs and bare feet, and her arms were thin and stringy, and her hair was matted and filthy. She was covered with years of dirt, so that she looked very brown. And when she raised her face, it was one of the most beautiful faces we have ever seen. Her eyes were crafty, like the eyes of a fox, but they were not human. The face was well developed, not moronic. Somewhere in the terror of the fighting in the city, something had snapped, and she had retired to some comfort of forgetfulness . . . . Her face was of chiseled loveliness, and on her long legs she moved with the grace of a wild animal . . . And as she gnawed at a loaf of bread, one side of her ragged filthy shawl slipped away from her dirty young breast, and her hand automatically brought the shawl back and covered her breast, and patted it in place with a heart-breaking feminine gesture . . . . It was a face to dream about for a long time (Steinbeck, 1999, 115-118).

CHAPTER EIGHTEEN

Final Punctuation: Psyche-in-Flesh

The key phenomena of this book are touch and vision. They are part and parcel of all forms of sensuality-sexuality. Sight and touch, the eye and the hand, are also bodily. But in what sense are they embodied? Rather than just take seeing and touching for granted, this little chapter digs into the meaning of embodiment.

We are earthlings. I do not say that to be pedantic or condescending. We are incarnated. We are embodied subjects made of flesh and blood, skin, sinews, and bone. We are creatures of heart and mind, and of soul and spirit. We are passionately reflective and reflectively passionate. We are by no means sophisticated computers, highly evolved primates, cyborgs, or detached spirits. We live on this patch of good earth from which Death will claim us. We dwell in finite time, relentlessly becoming and changing. We are earthlings.

Embodiment: Philosophical Roots

Nihilism plagues western philosophy. Nihilism means a way of thinking that is life-denying or death-embracing. In our culture's ruling rational, positive, natural science psychology, nihilism shows in a dread of warm flesh, the living body, and the fear of passion and tenderness. Historically and still, carnal desire befuddles normal science and technology. They simply cannot incorporate into their models the spontaneous blaze of hot flesh. Mainstream psychology basically ignores the phenomena that comprise this book.

Platonic Christendom

Plato, a "coward before reality" according to Nietzsche, trucks nihilism into western thought. For 2,500 years, his elegantly poetic dialogues have thrown a death shroud over the earth. For Platonism, be-coming has no real existence; earthy life counts for nothing; time is merely the moving image of eternity. Alleged ideal eternal forms are the privileged 'real'. Our pre-existing souls, "trailing clouds of glory," plop into our body and crash land into a Cave. We wayfarers find temporary abode in a vale of tears, this ground upon which I walk. Home is somewhere beyond.

Chained, facing a wall, and watching shadows flicker we cannot turn to see the light. Our lying eyes deceive us. The beautiful panorama is merely a *simulated scene*. Ideas, grasped through reason, alone yield truth. This warped abstract vision despises, denigrates, and demeans our individualized, deathbound *mortal flesh*. Platonic-Christendom considers the body a corruptible shell, a container of evil lusts that imprisons the eternal spirit.

Pertinent to the themes of this book, Platonic thought has held the body in *contempt*. Platonism dreads and detests the upsurge of carnal delight: murmurs, and sighs; the scent of bodily fluids and the smell of body odors; the visual lures of eye-talk and finger-talk: the warmth of touching caressing petting rubbing kneading squeezing scratching nibbling biting cuddling snuggling.

The narratives and reflections in this book turn 180 degrees away from such an abstract, arbitrary ideology and from other—worldly blather. My approach aims to resurrect the body as our vital subjectivity. What is our body? Or more precisely, how does it figure into our experience of the world? How does it fit into making sense out of that experience? And how is it even implicated in actually co-organizing it?

My living body is not a thing in the sense that a frog is a thing, or a fish is, or a stone. Why not? My body is a subject, that's why. It is an active agent. My body is me. I have my body, yes, but I also am my body. It is not like something I witness moving in the water, or poised on the riverbank; it is not like what I spot lodged inert in the dirt adjacent to the frog. When I touch my flesh,

I experience a double. It is different than what I sense when I catch the hopping frog and clutch it in my hands, feeling its warm life quivering. And it's different than the feel of digging out and fingering the cold, dirty, rough rock. How is it different? When I clasp my own hand, I feel the density and solidity and force of my own flesh; my own warmth comes back to me. I feel me, not a soft vegetable specimen like broccoli, or either a squishy frog or furry hamster. I touch my embodied consciousness that is me as an intentional co-creator of meaning.

Perform a simple experiment. Touch your desk; feel its external hard coldness. Ask permission to touch the hand of the person sitting next to you. Absorb her soft warmth. Then, fold your own hands, as if to pray. In the latter act, you are both giver and the receiver of the heat. You are a seen-seer, a touching-touched. In such a simple act, I sense my spirit-in-skin, a very personal example of incarnation: the word made flesh. Double sentience, Merleau-Ponty (1962) calls it. Incarnation is inspirited, never reducible to brute materiality. The human body does not just decoratively clothe the mind. Embodiment is a *reflexive structure*. Detached reason is a myth.

My body is not an idea either. When I stop thinking about it, it does not drift away. I might conceptualize it as thinner, lovelier, or more muscular, but my two peepers see on it or in the mirror the spare tire around my tummy, my too crooked nose, and two flabby arms.

Nor is my body reducible to a biological wonder, a product of Darwin's misguided mechanistic evolution. My body is my rich and vital history. I grew up on the prairies. I developed early. I indulged myself in sweets and junk food. I did time, too, as a couch potato. I dieted religiously, keeping keenly abreast of each new promising fad. I visited a tattoo parlor and slept with the stylist whose needle probed at the entrance to my Delta of Venus. I cut my own hair, an act of angry depression. That's my run-of-the-mill tale of madness, my adventures in and with my living flesh. It's me!

My body is a *thing I have* (anatomically and physiologically subject to physical laws of gravity and to vital laws of respiration, digestion, and sexual reproduction and also a *medium of culture.* And it is the *subject* I am (co-determining imagination, creativity and choice). We saw that at puberty, the change in body in both meanings is pivotal to understanding the lust dynamism and the mystery of sensuality-sexuality. Our lived body is an *object* of observation for-the-other, an ambiguous meaning-creating *subject* for me. My body is 'a general medium for having the world, a power to take root in different situations . . . of gaining structures of conduct' (Merleau-Ponty, 1962, 146; 158). The lived body "knows" the sensible world better than the conscious 'I':

> The blind man's stick has ceased to be an object for him . . . . its point has become an area of sensitivity, extending the scope and active radius of touch, and providing a parallel to sight; the French woman wearing her favorite hat with a long feather glides through the doorway without any calculation . . . . She feels where the feather is just as we feel where our hand is (Merleau-Ponty, 1962, 143).

Mundane realities are our common lot. We ache, break, bleed, and cry real tears. We smile and giggle, sweat and spit, belch, fart, and blow our noses. Preeminently social beings that are never out of relationships, we avoid picking our noises in front of others. We cover our mouths whenever we cough and most definitely cover up while sneezing. In anger, we shake our fists in protest or flip the finger in futile rage when feeling violated. Grief-stricken we rant, rave, and shriek curses to high heaven. We kiss someone and end up with a tongue in our mouth, saliva on our chin, a bite mark on our neck, and staring at a wet stain on the sheet. We are earthlings.

REFERENCES

Alapack, R. J. 1972. The phenomenology of the natural athlete. *Dissertation Abstracts International* (University Microfilms, No. 73-14, 658).

Alapack, R. J. 1975. The outlaw relationship: An existential phenomenological reflection upon the transition from adolescence to adulthood. In A. Giorgi, C. Fischer, & E.' Murray (Eds.); *Duquesne Studies in Phenomenological Psychology, II.* Pittsburgh: Duquesne University Press.

Alapack, R. J. 1984. Adolescent first love. In C.M. Aanstoos (Ed.), *Studies in the social sciences: Vol. 23. Exploring the Lived World: Readings in Phenomenological Psychology (pp.* 101-117). Carrollton: West Georgia College.

Alapack, R. J. 1986 May. Adolescent first kiss, presented to the Fifth International Human Science Research Conference, the University of California, Berkely, CA,

Alapack, R. J. 1987 June. Adolescent marks and stains: A Kierkegaardian quickened reflection. Paper presented at the Sixth International Human Science Research Conference, University of Ottawa, Ottawa, Ontario, Canada

Alapack, R.J. 1991a. Adolescent first kiss. *The Humanistic Psychologist.* 19(1), 48-67.

Alapack, R. J. 1991b. Malignant currency: The psychosocial aftershocks of the Exxon Valdez oil hemorrhage in the lived world of Seward, Alaska. In C. Aanstoos (Ed.), *Studies in humanistic psychology, Vol. 29* (pp. 134-52). Carrollton, GA: West Georgia College Studies in the Social Sciences.

Alapack, R.J. 1993. Harbinger of violence: A young woman's first kiss. In N. J. Mc Candless (Ed.), *Women: Contemporary Issues and Perspectives*, 31, (pp. 51-59). Carrollton, GA: West Georgia Studies in the Social Sciences.

Alapack, R. J. 1997 August. Technology and the body: Vanishing hickeys and the waning of adolescence. Presented to the Sixteenth International Human Science Research Conference, Trondheim, Norway.

Alapack, R. J. 2001. Sketches on human love, sexuality, and sensuality. Psykologisk Tidsskrift. *1, 4-10*

Alapack, R.J., M. Flydal Blichfeldt, and Å. Elden. 2005. Flirting on the Internet and the hickey: A Hermeneutic. *CyberPsychology & Behavior* 8(1), 52-61

Alapack, R. J. 2006 November. Flirting on the Internet and the Blush, the Kiss, the Hickey and the Caress: A Hermeneutic. Presented to the 4th *International Conference Cyperspace*, Masyryk University, Brno, The Czech Republic.

Alapack, R. J. 2007. *Love's pivotal relationships: The chum, first love, outlaw, and the intimate partner.* Central Milton Keynes, England: AuthorHouse.

Alapack, R. J. 2009. The epiphany of female flesh: A phenomenological hermeneutic of popular fashion. *Journal of Popular Culture*, 42 (6), 977-1003.

Alapack, R. J. 2010a. *Sorrow's profiles: Death, grief and crisis in the family*. London: Karnac.

Alapack, R. J. 2010b. *White hot-true blue: Psychological parables, narratives, and eye-witness accounts*. Indianapolis: Xlibris Corporation.

Alapack, R. J. 2011. Under siege: A woman's beauty and health. *The Humanistic Psychologist*, **39**(04), pp. 366-374.

Artaud, A. 1965. Van Gogh: The man suicided by society. In J. Hirschman (Ed.) *Antonin Artaud: Anthology*, 35-163. San Francisco: City Lights Books. (Orig. pub. French 1956)

Baker. O. 2002. Belly-baring jeans work their way back up: Women are getting hip to modest waistlines. *USA Today*. 4August: B1.

Balsamo, A. 1996. Forms of technological embodiment: Reading the body in contemporary culture. In *Cyberspace /Cyberbodies /Cyberpunk*. M. Featherrtstone & R. Burrows (Eds.).

Barthes, Ronald. 1991. *The pleasure of the text*. New York: The Noonday Press.

Baudrillard, J. 1988. *Selected writings*. Cambridge: Polity Press.

Binswagner, L. 1958. The case of Ellen West. In R. May, E. Angel and H. F. Ellenberger (Eds. & Trans.). *Existence*. 237-364. New York: A Clarion Book. (Orig. pub. 1944).

Buber, M. 1958. *I and Thou* (New York: Charles Scribner's Sons,

Bruner J. S., Sherwood V. 1976. Peekaboo and the learning of rule structures. In J. S. Bruner, A. Jolly, & K. Sylva (Eds.), *Play: Its role in development and evolution*, 277-285. New York: Basic Books.

Casado i Marin, L. C. 2000. Identity, emotions and the language of the body: Readings and meanings of bodily self-harm in young people. *Medische Anthropologie*, 21 (1), 75-92.

Chermin, K. 1981. *The obsession: Reflections on the tyranny of slenderness*. New York: Harper & Row.

Chesterton, G.K.1957. *St.Francis of Assisi*. New York: Doubleday (Orig. pub.1924)

Cornelissen, R. 1997. The situational vortex: A Phenomenological interpretation. Unpublished Manuscript, Art Institute of Pittsburgh, Pittsburgh, PA.

Edmonds, A. 2008. Beauty and health: Anthropological perspectives. *Medische Anthropologie* 20 (1) 151-62.

Edmonds, A. 2008. Beauty, health, and risk in Brazilian plastic surgery. *Medische Anthropologie* 21 (1) 21-38.

Edmonds, A., and S. van der Geest 2009. Introducing beauty and health. *Medische Anthropologie* 21 (1): 5-19

Eliot, T.S. 1963. The rock In: *The four quartets: Collected poems 1909-1962,* 161. London : Farber and Farber. (Orig. pub. 1936)

Elkin, H. 1966. Love and violence: A psychoanalytic viewpoint, *Humanitas: Journal of the Institute of man. II*: 168-169.

Elkin, H. 1972. Selfhood and ego structures. The Psychoanalytic Review, 59 (3), 389-416.

Erikson, E. 1959. *Identity and the life cycle.* New York: International universities Press.

Fernald A., and D. K. O'Neill 1993. Peekaboo across cultures: How mothers and infants play with voices, faces, and expectations. In K. MacDonald (Ed.), Parent-child play: Descriptions and implications (259-285). Albany: State University of New York.

Fogel A., K. L., Dickson, H. Hus, D. Messinger, G. C. Melson-Goens, and E. Nwokah. 1997. Communication of smiling and laughter in mother-infant play: Research on emotion from a dynamic systems perspective. In D. Barrett (Ed.), The communication of emotion: Current research from diverse perspectives (New Directions for Child Development No. 77, pp. 5-24). San Francisco, CA: Jossey-Bass.

Fitzgerald, F.S. 1953. *The Great Gatsby.* New York: Scribner. (Orig. pub. 1925)

Fitzgerald; F. S. 1970. *This side of paradise.* New York: Scribner. (Orig. pub. 1920)

Foucault, M. 1979. *Discipline and punish.* Trans. A. Sheridan New York: Vintage Books. (Orig. pub. French 1975)

Freud, S. 1905d. *Three essays on the theory of sexuality.* S.E., 7: 123-245. London: Hogarth, 1953.

Giorgi, A. 1970. *Psychology as a human science.* New York: Harper & Row.

Giorgi, A. 2009. *The descriptive phenomenological method in psychology: A modified Husserlian approach.* Pittsburgh: Duquesne University Press.

Griffin, G. E. 2003. *A world without cancer: The story of Vitamin B-17.* 2nd New Ed. Rev. and updated. Westlake Village, CA: American Media.

Hall, Dennis 2001 May. Delight in disorder: A reading of diaphany and liquefaction in contemporary woman's clothing. *Journal of Popular Culture.*

Hamman, R. B. 1996. The role of fantasy in the construction of the On-line Other: A selection of interviews and participant observations from cyberspace. http://www.socio.demon.co.uk/fantasy/html

Heidegger, M. 1993. The end of philosophy and the task of thinking. In: D. F. Krell (Ed.), *Martin Heidegger: Basic Writings,* 431-449. San Francisco: HarperSanFrancisco. (Orig. pub. German 1969)

Hemingway, E. 1968. *For whom the bell tolls.* New York: Scribner. (Orig. pub. 1940)

Husserl, E. 1973. *The idea of phenomenology.* W. P. Alston and G. Hakhnikian (Trans.). The Hague: Martinus Nijhoff. (Orig. pub. German 1929)

Huizinga, J. 1955. *Homo ludens: A study of the play element in culture.* Boston: Beacon. (Orig. pub 1944).

Karakasidou, A. 2008. The elusive subversion of order: Cancer and the human experience in modern Crete, Greece. In J. McMullin & D. Weiner (Eds.), *Cultural perspectives on cancer: From metaphor to advocacy.* Santa Fe, New Mexico: School for American Research Press, pp. 83-102.

Kaw, E. 1993. Medicalization of racial features: Asian American women and cosmetic surgery. *Medical Anthropology Quarterly* 7 (1): 74-89.

Keel, P.K. and K. L. Klump. 2003. Are eating disorders culture-bound syndromes? Implications for conceptualizing their ideology. *Psychological Bulletin.*129.5 747-69.

Keen, E. 1975. *A primer in phenomenological psychology.* New York: Holt, Rinehart, and Winston.

Kierkegaard, S. 1971. The ancient tragical motif as reflected in the modern. In: *Either/Or, Vol. I.* (pp. 229-277). D. F. Swenson & L. M. Swenson (Trans.). Princeton, NJ; Princeton University Press. (Orig. pub. Danish 1843)

Kierkegaard, S. 1980. *The concept of anxiety.* Princeton, N.J.: Princeton University Press. (Orig. pub. Danish 1844)

King, C. R. 1996. The siren scream of telesex: Speech, seduction and simulation. *Journal of Popular Culture;* 30: 91-101.

Klein, M. 1975. The development of a child. In: M. Klein *Love, guilt and reparation & other works 1921-1945.* London: The Hogarth Press (Original pub. 1921)

Kruger, H. 1982. *A crack in the wall: Growing up under* Hitler. Hein, R. Tran. New York: Fromm International Publishing Corporation (Orig. pub. German 1966)

Lacan, J. 1977. The mirror stage as formative of the function of the I as revealed in psychoanalytic experience. In *Ecrits: A selection.* New York: W.W. Norton. (Orig. pub. French 1949)

Lawrence, D. H. 1975. *The rainbow.* New York: Viking. (Orig. pub.1915)

Lawrence, D. H. 1976. The shades of spring. In *The complete short stories: Vol. I.*, 131-147. New York: Penguin Books.

Lawrence, D. H. 1981. *Fantasia of the unconscious/ Psychoanalysis and the unconscious.* New York: Penguin Books. (Orig. pub. 1921)

Lawrence, D. H. 1983. *Lady Chatterley's lover.* (Preface, L. Durrell; Ed. & Intro., R. Friedland. Toronto: Bantam Books. The complete and unexpurgated Orioli Edition. (Orig. pub. 1928)

Laye, C. 1964. *The African child: Memories of a West African childhood.* London: Fontana Books (Orig. pub. French 1954)

Levinas, E. 1969. *Totality and infinity: An essay on exteriority* (A. Lingis, Trans.). Pittsburgh: Duquesne University Press (Orig. pub. French 1961)

Levinas, E. 1996. *Proper names.* (M. B. Smith, Trans.). Stanford, CA: Stanford University Press. (Orig. pub. French 1975)

Lingis, A. 1983. *Excesses: Eros and culture.* Albany, New York: State University of New York Press.

Lingis, A. 1985. *Libido: The French existential theories.* Indianapolis: Indiana University Press.

Lingis, A. 2011. *Violence and splendor.* Evanston: Ill: Northwestern University Press.

Lynch, J. J. 1985. *The language of the heart: The body's response to human dialogue.* New York: Basic Books.

Mac Cormack, P. 2006 May. The great ephemeral tattooed skin. *Body and Society* 12:2, 57-82.

Maugham, W. S. 1982. *Of human bondage*. New York: Penguin. (Orig. pub. 1919).

Merleau-Ponty, M. 1962. *The phenomenology of perception*. (C. Smith, Trans.). London: Routledge & Kegan Paul.

Mishima, Yukio 1973. *Spring snow*. (M. Gallagher, Trans.). New York: Pocket Books.

Money, J. 1986. *Lovemaps*. New York: Irvington Publishers, Inc.

Montague, D., and A. S Walker-Andrews. 2001. Peekaboo: A new look at infants' perception of emotion expression, *Developmental Psychology*, 37, November, 2001. 6. 826; 831.

Nietzsche, F. 1982. Twilight of the idols. In W. Kaufmann (Ed. and Trans.). *The Portable Nietzsche*, 463-563). New York: Penguin Books. (Orig. pub. German 1889).

Nietzsche, F. 1955. *Beyond god and evil*. M. Cowen, Trans. and Intro.). Chicago: Gateway Edition (Orig. pub. German 1855)

Ogino M., T. Ooide, A. Watanabe, and M. Asada. 2007. Acquiring peekaboo communication: Early communication model based on reward prediction. *IEEE*. 116-121.

O'Hallaren, B. 1976. Stop the chase—It's time for my comb out. *TV Guide*, 25 September, 25-30.

Parrott W. G. and H. Gleitman. Infant's expectations in play: The joy of peek-a-boo., *Cognition and Emotion*, 3, 1989, 291-311

Perella, N. J. 1969. *The kiss sacred and profane*. Los Angeles, CA: University of California Press.

Phillips, R. 1967. Children's games. In R. Slovenko, and J. A. Knight *Motivation in play, games, and sports.* Springfield: Ill.: Charles C. Thomas.

Piaget, J. 1992. *Origins of intelligence in children* (New York: International Universities Press. (Orig. pub. French 1936).

Pearce, D. 2011, 20 August). "I'm injecting my eight-year-old with Botox and getting her body waxes so she'll be a superstar." *The Sun*, 1-2.

Pompa, Y. 1999. *Barbie: Totally cool nail party.* New York: Reader's Digest Books.

Raddall, T. H. 1982. *The nymph and the lamp.* Toronto: McClelland & Stewart. (Orig. pub. 1963)

Roberts, C. 2003. The politics of Farrah's body: The feminine icon as cultural embodiment. *The Journal of Popular Culture.* 37, 1, 83-104.

Rogers, M. F. 1999. *Barbie culture.* London: Sage Publications.

Rubin, T. 1977. *Coming out.* New York: Pocket Books. (Orig. pub.1967)

Rupp, S. 2004. Plumbing the history of the new cleavage. The Tyee.ca. Feb. 2004. The Tyee.ca 14 Mar. 2005 (http://www.geocities?joanprovoc/string.html?200514).

Rutherfurd, E.1992 *Russka.* New York: Ivy Books.

Sartre, J-P. 1976. The childhood of a leader. In *Intimacy.* New York: New Directions. (Orig. pub. French 1948)

Sartre, J-P. 1966. *Being and nothingness: A Phenomenological essay on ontology.* H. E. Barnes (Trans.). New York: Washington Square Press (Orig. pub. French 1943).

Schutz, 1971, *Collected papers. Volume II.* The Hague: Martinus Nijtoff. 37-62.

Shakespeare, W. 1980. Romeo and Juliet. In *The complete works of William Shakespeare.* London: Octopus Books. (Orig. pub. 1595)

Spitz, R.1965. *The first-year of life.* New York: International Universities Press, Inc.

Stang, R. 1979. *Edvard Munch.* New York: Abbeville Press.

Steinbeck, J. 1999. *A Russian journal.*, Photographer R, Capa. New York: Penguin.

Steinbeck, J. 1947. *The wayward bus.* New York: The Viking Press.

Sullivan, H. S. 1953. *The interpersonal theory of psychiatry.* New York: Norton.

Stoker, B. 1992. *Dracula.* New York: Signet. (Orig. pub. 1897)

Taylor, E. 2005. Oscar at 77: Film, fashion, warm bodies. *LA Weekly* March 4-10, 2005, p. 10.

Tiefer, L. 2000. Sexology and the pharmaceutical industry: The threat of co-optation. *Journal of Sex Research*, 37 (3), 273-283.

Tiefer, L. 2011 April. *Is sex more like dancing or digestion? How a paradigm affects research, education and practice.* Keynote address presented at Women's Health: Science, Technology, and Society, St. Francis College, Brooklyn Heights, New York.

Twiggy. www.swingchicks.com/twiggy.htm 3/14/2005.

Van den Berg, J. H. 1961. *The changing nature of man.* New York: Dell Publishing Co.

Van den Berg, J. H. 1972. *Different Existence: Principles of phenomenological psychopathology.* Pittsburgh: Duquesne University Press.

Van Gennep, A. 1975. *The rites of passage.* M.B. Vizedom and G.L. Caffee (Trans.) and S.T. Kimball (Intro.). Chicago: The University of Chicago Press (Orig. pub. Dutch 1908

Weitman, S. 1999. On the elementary forms of socioerotic life. pp. 71-110. In: M. Featherstone (Ed.), *Love & Eroticism.* London: Sage.

Whiting, J. W. M., R. P. Kluckhohn, and A. S. Anthony. 1958. The function of male initiation ceremonies at puberty. In E. E. Maccoby, T. M. Newcomb, and E. L. Hartley, (Eds.). *Readings in social psychology* (3d ed.), 359-370. New York: Henry Holt and Company.

Weitz, Rose. 1998. Ed. *The politics of women's bodies: Sexuality, appearance, and behavior.* Oxford: Oxford University Press.

Wertz, F. J. 1986. The rat in psychological science. *The Humanistic Psychologist.* 14(3), 143-68.

Winnicott, D.W. 1953.Transitional objects and transitional phenomena—a study of the first not-me possession. *International Journal of Psycho-Analysis,* 24: 89-97.

Winnicott, D.W. The capacity to be alone. In D.W. Winnicott, *The maturational processes and the facilitating environment,* 29-36). London: Karnac. (Orig. pub.1965)